BETWEEN PLACES

LUW PRESS · SALT LAKE CITY, UTAH

BETWEEN PLACES

A Collection of Prose & Poetry

ISBN-13: 978-0988236721 (LUW Press)
ISBN-10: 0988236729

Book format and cover design by Mark E. Moody.

CONTENTS

BETWEEN PLACES

Amanda Yardley Luzzader

JESSIE KNEW BEFORE I DID. "AS SOON AS THE DOOR OPENED," she told me later.

Mom came home early that day. She walked in without seeming to notice us and headed straight for her bedroom. All three of us girls followed her, and we watched as she rummaged through a dresser drawer. She unearthed a cigarette—must have squirreled it away when she quit smoking a while back. It quivered between her lips as she lit up. Then, she closed her eyes and took a long drag, holding the burn inside for a moment before releasing it in a slow smoky sigh.

And then I knew, too.

Seven jobs in two years.

The next week I found myself in the backseat of our old Chevy with my older sister Jessie on one side and my younger sister Liza on the other. Our feet competed for space amongst the duffle bags and grocery sacks in which we'd packed all our possessions.

"How long are we going to stay there?" Liza, she's five, had sunk in her seat until the lap portion of her seatbelt rested near her armpits.

"Not long," Mom answered. "Just while we're in-between places."

"How come you're not staying?" Liza had asked this a half-dozen times, but she kept asking as if she hoped the answer might change.

Mom sighed. "I need some time alone to figure things out. You guys shouldn't have to deal with my problems."

"Where will you go?" Jessie asked.

"I dunno. Maybe California. Somewhere along the coast."

Hours later, the sun was settling behind the mountains when our car finally hiccupped over the train tracks in my grandparents' town.

"Can we ride the train to come see you?" I asked.

"I won't be gone that long." Mom glanced back at me through the rearview mirror. "Besides, these tracks aren't really used by passenger trains anymore. They're mostly used for freight."

"What's freight?" Liza asked.

"It's like baggage," Jessie said. "Clothes and stuff."

"Could be anything really," Mom said. "Anything that needs to get somewhere."

When we finally arrived, Grandma hugged us at the door, a cough drop clicking against her teeth as she rolled it from cheek to cheek. While Grandpa went outside with Mom to get our things, Grandma told us where we'd be sleeping. Since Liza was the youngest, she would sleep in the room next door to Grandma and Grandpa, in case she got scared. Jessie and I would share the guest room in the basement.

"You'll have to make your own beds," Grandma said. "My hip's too bad to go downstairs anymore."

Even though we'd visited plenty of times before, Jessie and I raced downstairs to inspect our new room. Jessie was two years older than me, but she never acted bossy or superior. Before we had even reached the bottom step, we were already pretending to be roommates renting our first place. Technically, Jessie was only my half sister, but she seemed more than whole to me. I didn't even mind sharing the queen bed with her.

Our assigned room smelled like an old library stocked with potatoes. A water pipe ran along one of the walls, and when it sang, I'd wrap my hand around it to see if the water was hot or cold. The carpet was pink, and wood paneling lined the walls.

Jessie and I were trying out the bed by lying on it when Mom appeared in the doorway. She had her purse in one hand and her keys in the other. Jessie and I both sat up.

"This will be nice." Mom looked around the room as though she'd never seen it before. "I'm about to go," she said, "come give me a hug."

Jessie scampered off the bed to embrace her, but I didn't move.

"Aren't you going to hug me good-bye?" she asked with one arm draped over Jessie. There was a hurt in her eyes that guilted me. I crawled off the bed, and then hugged her tightly at her waist. I kept hugging her and hugging her until she finally stuck her arm between us and pried me away.

"Tell me when you're coming back," I said.

Mom looked up as she considered the question. "August twentieth," she finally said. "I'll be back the twentieth."

After she left, I begged Grandma to get the calendar down. The twentieth was nearly six weeks away.

"I'm going to mark each day until she comes back," I said.

"No, I'm going to," Jessie said.

"What about me?" Liza asked.

Grandma found three different colored pens—red for me, blue for Jessie, and green for Liza—and every morning we'd each cross the day off in our own colored pen.

While we kept careful track of the days, it was harder to track smaller units of time. Grandma and Grandpa didn't use any clocks. I never even saw one in the house. Instead, they listened for train whistles. A train told us when it was time for lunch and another one for dinner. A whistle call late in the afternoon told Grandpa when to stop working, and the train that chased the sunlight signaled the time for bed. The red-eye came through around 6 a.m., and though I seldom heard it, it woke Grandma and Grandpa each day. We were accustomed to finding them already dressed, fed, and waiting for us in the kitchen when we finally rolled out of bed.

One morning, I awoke alone; Jessie had already gotten up. The white curtains over the window glowed with sunlight as birds whistled outside. I felt so relaxed, still wrapped in the thin quilt and sheets, that I didn't want to get up. I just stayed there, wondering where Mom was and what she was doing. I pictured her at the beach, the wind blowing her wavy hair as she waded into the water. My eyes meandered around the room while I daydreamed, and suddenly I saw a man's face.

He was in the paneling next to the light switch. The wood grain swirled perfectly to make the outline of a rounded beard and a pointy nose. And in addition to his slight frown and droopy eyes, something about him looked sad. I felt like crying when I saw him. I couldn't help but think he hadn't wanted to be part of wood paneling in a dank basement. Out of all the things he could have been—a throne, a rocking horse, a nativity set—it must have been disappointing to end up as nothing more than a spot on the wall.

At first, I'd have to search for his face, but after a few weeks, I couldn't not see him. I'd squint to see if I could change him back to wood, back to grain. But each time I'd leave the room, his eyes followed me.

On August thirteenth, I walked upstairs to find Jessie helping Grandma fry eggs and toast bread. Grandpa had donned his reading glasses and was perusing the paper while Liza sat in a chair kicking the table. I stood in front of the calendar with my red pen, as I did each morning. Liza's green x's had stopped appearing weeks ago, and Jessie's blue marks stopped shortly after that, making it my job to mark the dates leading up to Mom's return. By that time, Mom's phone calls had dwindled from every day to every other day and then down to once a week. But as I crossed off the day, I noticed the date boldly circled (in three different colors) was only a week away, and my heart fluttered.

I sat in a chair next to Liza and stared out the window at the distant miles of train tracks passing through the fields. I always hoped to see a train while we were waiting for breakfast, but I never did. My grandparents told me that I'd never see one at that time because the trains always stayed on schedule. I wanted them to be wrong. I checked every day, but the tracks were always still and silent—lonely in the interim.

"Do the trains here go to California?" I asked.

"Of course," Grandpa said. "Trains can go anywhere there are tracks. These ones connect all the way from Sacramento to Tallahassee. That's clear across the country."

"But they only go on their route," Grandma said. "They can't just go wherever they want, they have to go where they're expected, and I'm not sure that the trains she's seeing go to California."

Grandma set a plate piled high with toast on the table, and Liza lifted the corner of the top piece with her pinkie. "Grandma, you burnt the toast."

"Eat up," Grandpa said, "It'll put some hair on your chest."

"I don't want hair on my chest," Liza mumbled.

Grandpa folded his glasses and put them in his shirt pocket. "Do you girls know I brought your Grandma here on the train?"

We did, but we loved to hear him tell the story.

"When was that?" Jessie asked as she pulled up a chair.

"Right after the war, I decided I needed to find a wife. So, I went to the city, found the prettiest gal there, married her, and brought her home. Easy as that."

"I wouldn't have come if I'd known I was coming to this," Grandma said.

Grandpa covered his mouth with his hand, but then whispered loudly, "I wouldn't have brought her if I'd known she'd turn into that."

Grandma hurled a hot pad at Grandpa's head and he laughed.

I tried to picture what Grandma must have looked like when she arrived on the train, back before the wrinkles and extra pounds. The best I could come up with was a life-sized cutout of her black-and-white senior picture that hung in the hall. I imagined Grandpa stepping off the train, and then turning around to help the two-dimensional beauty down the steps and leading her to her new home. In my mind, her picture with its frozen smile, donned an apron and spent the rest of its days farming, washing laundry, cooking and raising six photo paper children. If Grandma had really known what her future held, I wonder if she still would have boarded that train.

"Hey, look! There's Meanie!" Liza jumped from her seat and ran to the window.

None of Grandpa's barn cats were particularly friendly, but Meanie was the white cat from hell. We could sometimes pet the other cats if we got them cornered, but not Meanie. She'd arch her back and puff up so big her tail would look like a raccoon's. Then, she'd bare her teeth while hissing and spitting. If we still didn't leave, she'd fold her ears back and a scream would escape her open mouth, as if our mere presence was exorcising some demon within.

"Her kittens should be getting big enough that she'll bring 'em down soon," Grandpa said.

When the time came for Meanie to have her kittens, she'd climbed up to the rafters of Grandpa's barn—too high for us to see her babies.

"Why'd she have them up there anyway?" Liza asked.

"Probably to keep them away from you." Grandpa laughed.

"She'll either bring them down soon or they'll fall and break their necks," Grandma said.

Grandma's comment had us girls going to the barn every day looking for raining kittens so we could rescue them. Sometimes we heard mewing, and we'd stretch our hands above our heads hoping to catch them. Grandpa would walk by and say, "Just promise me you won't handle them too much. They'll get soft and won't make good mousers if you touch them too much."

The week passed with no sight of kittens, but by then we had other things to think about. On August twentieth, we girls unrolled several feet of butcher paper in the driveway. Jessie brought out her portable radio and while the Beach Boys sang, "I wish they all could be California girls," we decorated the banner for Mom.

I wanted it to say, *Welcome Home Mom!* but Jessie said we needed to write *Welcome Back* since this wasn't really our home. We settled on *Welcome Mom! We missed you!* but we ran out of room for the longer phrase and had to write the "you" in small print vertically at the end of the sign. Using crayons and markers we added hearts, stars, and rainbows to the banner. The texture of the cement pressed through the paper where we drew, and Liza ripped a small hole on the left side, but it still looked pretty good. When we were done, Grandpa got out his ladder and hung the banner outside above the front window.

"She'll be able to see it from a mile away." He smiled.

We girls went inside and stood at the window, watching for our car to bring Mom back to us.

"A watched pot never boils," Grandma said, and she ushered us outside to play. As I ducked out the back door, I caught her looking out the window herself, staring down the road.

A little while later, Grandpa asked me to go grocery shopping with him.

"What should we get to eat to celebrate your Mom coming back," he asked as he pushed the cart past the milk aisle.

I almost said sausage dogs, 'cause they're my favorite, but then I thought about Mom and decided to get her favorites instead. We bought ribs, corn on the cob, potatoes, and a nice, big watermelon.

Long after the evening train's whistle sounded, we girls sat on the couch with our pajamas on and our teeth brushed. Grandma sat in her rocking chair holding her old rotary phone on her lap as the chirps of crickets floated through an open window.

"I guess we oughta get you girls to bed," Grandpa said.

Liza's eyes were already drooping and she didn't seem to be aware of anything. Jessie and I looked to Grandma as Grandpa carried Liza to her bed.

"Well, who knows when she'll get here," Grandma said. "Just get to bed, and we can all have breakfast together in the morning."

We went downstairs and lay in our bed. I tried to stay awake in the darkness, ears straining to hear the car's motor or the front door open, but despite my resistance, I fell asleep.

Jessie and I woke up at about the same time. We looked at each other, and then flew upstairs, but when we got there, we only saw Grandma and Grandpa.

"She isn't here," Grandma said. The wrinkles on her face looked deeper. She wrung a tissue in her hands. "I just hope she's held up somewhere and hasn't gotten in some accident."

It rained that day in big swollen drops. The water dripped off the roof and emptied from the rain spout like a faucet. Jessie, Liza, and I stood in Grandma's living room in front of the window, watching the rain and checking the road. The raindrops made the marker run on our banner. The colors swirled and dripped off the sign like colored tears.

Grandma stepped behind us and gazed over our heads and out the window. She walked away silently, and then suddenly appeared outside the window in the rain, without her jacket. She lifted her kitchen broom with both arms and swatted at the banner as her underarms shook. The paper ripped, part of it wrapping around the broom. She lowered her arms, and the entire banner fell to the ground. She looked up at the window—we made eye contact for a just a moment—and then she turned and walked back toward the garage.

All three of us ran to meet her at the door. When she swung it open and saw us, she stepped back in surprise. The rain had drenched her clothing; I could see her bra through her plaid shirt. She stepped past us, still holding the broom.

"We'll make a new one tomorrow," she said.

Grandma and Grandpa spent a lot of time on the phone. I kept marking the calendar. I couldn't shake the feeling that if one of us didn't cross off the days, Mom would never come back.

A few days after the rainstorm, we were playing UNO downstairs. I came up to get some graham crackers for a snack and overheard Grandma speaking sharply on the telephone.

"—School will be starting soon. You can't be like this when you have children. They need to have some stability—"

I ran back down the stairs, jumping over the last three steps.

"Grandma's talking to Mom!"

I turned and raced back up the stairs with my sisters at my heels.

We rushed to where Grandma was pacing with the receiver. She'd walk about five steps before the cord reached its limit, and then she'd turn and walk the opposite way. Grandma didn't even seem to notice we were there until she nearly collided with Liza.

"Call me tomorrow, and we'll figure it out. Your girls want to talk to you."

Grandma handed the receiver to Liza. "Hi, Mommy," she said cheerfully. Without giving our mother a chance to respond, Liza started telling her about the kittens in the barn.

"Where has she been?" I asked Grandma while Liza talked. I'd had a nightmare that Mom had driven our old Chevy off a cliff and into the Pacific Ocean.

Grandma shook her head slightly. "She's just been busy, that's all. Nothing to worry about."

Liza didn't stay on the phone long; Jessie took her turn next. After they talked for a while, Jessie handed the phone to me before heading back to the kitchen.

"Hello?"

"Hi, Sweetie! How are you doing?"

I wrapped the phone cord around my pinkie. "Fine."

"I knew you'd have so much fun there. But I miss you so much; I can't wait to see you girls again."

"When are you coming back?"

"Oh shoot, Honey! I can't really talk anymore. I'll call back tomorrow. Love you! Bye!"

The phone clicked before I even got to say good-bye. I stared at the receiver a moment, and when I looked up, I saw Grandma watching me. She took the handset from me and placed it back on the cradle.

"She sure seemed to miss you." Grandma smiled, but her eyes didn't wrinkle the way they normally did. "It'll only be a couple more days now."

When the train whistle blew for supper that evening, we sat down to a meal of ribs, corn on the cob, mashed potatoes, and watermelon for dessert.

After dinner, I went to my room to put on my shoes so I could check the barn again for kittens. But just as I was leaving, the wood grain man caught my eye. Though I heard nothing, I sensed him calling me. Jessie walked in and caught me staring at him.

"What are you doing?"

"Who's that crazy artist that cut off his own ear?"

"Van Gogh?"

"Yeah. This mark looks like his face."

She moved beside me, both of us facing the wall.

"I don't see anything."

I pointed. "It's right here. See, his face is turned like this." I mimicked his pose, and even lowered my eyebrows and exaggerated a frown. "You don't see it?"

Jessie shook her head and walked out of the room.

The grain man was emboldened now, nearly coming out of the wall.

I found a pencil and I traced the lines, pressing so hard that lead dust sprinkled to the floor. I moved over and over the wood grain, bringing to life his eyes, his mouth, his nose, and especially his one ear.

When I finished, you couldn't even tell I'd traced it. It looked like something an adult had drawn. Like a Van Gogh. I stepped back admiring him; he wasn't just a part of the wall anymore. Now he was somebody.

Next to the face, I signed my name in big capital letters, knowing Jessie couldn't miss him now. I went outside to get her, and found her next door in front of Grandpa's barn. I forgot the drawing when I saw two kittens cradled close to her chest.

"You caught 'em?"

The kittens struggled in Jessie's arms; she could barely contain them.

"Here," she said. "Take one."

"Hi there little kitty. What's your name?" I cupped my hands under the kitten's soft creamy fur, holding him close to my stomach. The kitten purred and rubbed his head against my hand as I pet him. Even though he had the same coloring and similar markings, it was hard to believe something so precious had come from an animal so vile as old Meanie. I wondered if Meanie had once been like the kitten, and if the kitten was destined to be like Meanie.

I remembered what Grandpa had said about not handling the kittens too much or they wouldn't be good mousers. Meanie was a great mouser. I quickly stroked the kitten's fur and rubbed my cheek against his side.

"I don't care if you are a lousy mouser," I told him as I carried him back to the house.

Lying on our bed, I dangled my hair in front of the kitten and laughed as he swatted at it.

Liza heard me and ran in. "A kitten!" She gasped and jumped on the bed. "I want to play with it."

I scooped him up. "You can play with it when I'm done," I said.

She watched as I caressed the kitten's head.

"Can I have a turn now?"

"Not yet."

I nuzzled his nose, rubbed under his chin.

"You're not supposed to have pets in the house," she said.

"Shut up, Liza."

"When do I get to have a turn?"

I rubbed the cat's ears. Twirled its tail around my finger. Liza sighed and stamped out of the room.

But almost as soon as she left, the kitten began mewing. It became unruly, slipping through my arms, rolling away from my hands.

"There, there, kitty. She's gone now. Don't worry I'll take care of you."

The mewing continued.

The kitten escaped my grasp, jumping to the bed where it stood in a very strange stance.

Uh-oh.

I smelled it before I saw it.

"On the bedspread?" My grandmother with her arthritic hip loomed at the doorway, a scowl deepening her wrinkles. Liza stood at her side. "Get that cat out of here before I wring its little neck."

She turned to leave the room, and as she did, she saw it. My masterpiece. My Van Gogh. From behind her, I watched her fingers curl into fists. She pounded the wall three times. "Dammit, dammit, dammit."

She whipped back. "You're ruining my house. You're ruining everything! You're just like your mother!"

I picked up the kitten, ducked past Grandma, and ran up the stairs two at a time. Grandma was your standard-issue, cookie-baking, choir-singing, white-haired grandma. I didn't know she could swear. Her words reverberated in my mind.

In the backyard, the swinging gate's old hinges squeaked as I stepped into Grandpa's farmland. The kitten freed itself from my arms as I reached the barn, but I kept walking.

My bare feet curled around hardened lumps of soil. Strings from my cut-off shorts tickled my knees.

The sun, lingering near the horizon, beckoned with yellow light that somehow seemed truer than that of noonday. The sun kissed the world with Midas lips. It converted my brown hair into shiny threads of Rumpelstiltskin gold, and warmed my pale skin.

I walked farther than I'd ever gone before, too far to hear shouts to come home, and still I walked. I walked until I reached the end of Grandpa's farm, marked by a crooked fence of sticks and barbed wire.

Beyond the fence, within a stone's throw, I saw pebbles leading to creosote-stained wooden ties and rusting railroad tracks. My eyes followed the line for miles, all the way to the center of town where a familiar, mustard-and-maroon Union Pacific engine stood parked with its line of freight.

Its whistle bellowed as the train lumbered down the tracks.

A calling came from within me.

Race the train.

My heart thumped inside my chest. I turned parallel to the tracks, waiting to start. The whistles sounded again. The ground vibrated. The tracks clanged.

The train sped past me, its thunder blowing through me. And then I ran—arms pumping, legs galloping. I watched the train with side-eyes, my hair a spiraling smoke trail behind me. The air tried to force me back, but I pushed through, and when the train dropped behind my view I knew it was chasing me. I was the conductor of my own train then, unbound by the limits of the tracks. I could go anywhere, see anything, and I ran, smiling, ahead of the train.

But then my feet slowed, and my arms dropped to my side. A perpendicular fence squared off Grandpa's property, stopping me in my footsteps. But there'd be no stopping the train. It barreled onward, snaking around turns, and climbing up hills, charging ahead to the places it was meant to go, stopping only at the places where it was expected to be. It left me behind, with the dust and the smoke—somewhere between places.

TÁ MHEIRICEÁ

Rodney Hurd

In dreams to hear the pluck of harp
and echo of the young swain's whistle
to sheep a grazin' in the glen.
Smell the meadowsweet in comin' rain,
see green hawthorn and thistle on the hill,
the white washed walls fenced by stone,
farms of Ó Cuilinn and Mac Domhnaill.
Yet these dreams exposed to realities light
were laid waste by landed noble's pride,
made the worst with potato's blight.
Land that could no more give what life required,
sent child to ship set off the coast
spreadin' canvas that would pass gray cliff
drawin' erstwhile kin to work new shores.
From the green of home gone to factory's gray,
abandonin' parish upon the knoll
where life recorded and began,
filled confessionals with struggle, hope,
now just crosses mark the end.
Only the children's children
with stories of days long past,
can open eyes, and cross themselves
take drink on the Feast of Saint Patrick's Day
though home be years and miles away
can breathe the breath and with a smile
dream of forgotten family and the Emerald Isle.

WELCOME TO THE FAMILY

Tim Keller

I HATE FUNERALS, ALWAYS HAVE. MOM AND DAD'S GENERATION, they love the things, or seem to anyway. Oh, there are always the tears, the exchange of sympathies, everything you'd expect. But phrases like: "If it weren't for funerals, we wouldn't see each other at all," imply a certain level of enjoyment. Not fair I know, but when you've attended as many funerals as I have, you can't help but be a little jaded.

See, my parents are possessed of talents very much in demand for occasions like church meetings, firesides, and especially funerals; be they of family, friends, or distant acquaintances.

Blessed with a beautiful singing voice and a talent for the piano, Mom is the entertainment. She can sing and if necessary, play a vast repertoire of hymns on demand, including but not limited to "Amazing Grace," "Nearer My God to Thee," "What a Friend we Have in Jesus," and the all-time requested favorite, "Softly and Tenderly—Jesus is Calling."

Dad on the other hand, is a gifted orator; he's been on the high council since before I was born, and thus has a great deal of speaking experience. His jokes are funny, and his metaphors always tie into his sermons. That alone sets him apart from the *run of the mill* high councilman; but those attributes do not, in and of themselves, account for his unique from of celebrity.

Dad has great intuition; he can always be counted on to relate that one funny tale, followed without fail, by another story guaranteed to mist the eyes of everyone in attendance, including, I'm sure, the deceased. But that's not entirely it either.

No, for my money, it's Dad's mission experience that started him down this road. He served a two-year mission in depression era Georgia, surrounded by Holy Rollers and Evangelical tent revivals. A place where religion is in the blood, and reverence is reviled as timidity. Where, if he wanted anyone to listen at all, he had to *walk the walk.*

Dad is a dynamic speaker. His vocal pitch varied, his body language animated; when the spirit takes him, and it frequently does—he moves, speaks, and preaches from its influence. Don't misunderstand, we're not talking about speaking in tongues, or rolling around the aisles, but pulpit pounding, congregation engaging interaction? You bet!

At the end of a typical service, Mom and Dad will be mobbed, thanked, and invariably asked *the question.*

"That was so beautiful," someone will say. "Will you sing/speak at my funeral?"

Of course they say "yes"; it's quite the honor after all. And for years, that honor meant my sister Shirlene and I would be attending as well; ostensibly to pay our respects, but often as not, to support the cast.

When adulthood arrived, my sister and I finally felt strong enough to beg off. In truth, Mom and Dad's fan base was such that we weren't even missed. And we still went to the important funerals, those of family, close friends, people we'd met more than once. Which is how we ended up at Uncle Lyle's funeral.

Lyle was our kind of people, good hearted, if a bit on the irreverent side. Besides, anyone who could indulge a seven decade love for unfiltered Lucky Strikes and make it to the ripe old age of eighty-six, deserved one hell of a send off.

The family gossip mill was rife with rumors of the sons and daughters duking it out over the inheritance. Compounding matters was ridiculous Mormon policy; namely that the boys, inactive for years, weren't allowed to participate in the funeral.

Strong opinions regarding that little tidbit echoed from the ward house Sunday School room, where moments before, the family prayer was held. The current ward Bishop was out of his league. Thankfully, Uncle Lyle's Bishop from years back had been asked to preside, and he was keeping the peace—barely. This sad little Thursday was shaping into a soap to put *Melrose Place* to shame.

For some inexplicable reason, the girls didn't ask Mom to sing, embarking instead on a musical program of their own. Eldest daughter, Lydia, once a violinist of some note, took to the stage to prove beyond doubt that the violin, while capable of producing the sweetest strains for the gifted and the dedicated, is in the hands of the hobbyist the least forgiving of all instruments.

Alas, Lydia fell into the latter category. The blending of notes most closely mirrored a toss up between fingernails on a chalkboard and tortured cat. Her performance made worse by the occasional memory of competence. Moments, few though they were, when the right amount of bow and string came together to mock us with the realization of what should have been "Amazing Grace."

My sister and I grasped hands, though we dared not look at each other, lest we dissolve into fits of hysterical laughter in the middle of our uncle's funeral.

Cousin Lydia, ever the trooper, stopped in the middle, wiped her tears and amazingly—began again! On and on it went, until finally, in a moment demonstrative of the adage that God hears and answers prayers, the song was over and the humiliated daughter fled to her seat.

Dad, stoic as any Vulcan, rose from his seat and approached the pulpit. A single glance toward the family section wilted any hint of a smile.

"Thank you Lydia, for that beautiful tribute to your father." he began—and Shirlene's Amazon grip nearly broke my hand.

"Oh, how Lyle loved that song. I remember when you were just a little girl. Your dad made sure that anyone visiting the house was treated to a recital, and no matter what songs you played, he always had you play that one. I can't think of a better way to honor him."

"Lyle was sixteen years older than me. That's quite a span. He was off to the army before I was out of short pants. He also worked for the forest service, and as a stevedore in Washington, so he didn't get back home very often. Every time he saw me though, he always made me feel like I was the most important person in the world."

"Lyle would've—" Dad stopped and gazed toward the back of the chapel, where the congregation turned, half expecting to see Lyle himself.

"When Lyle retired to Arizona," Dad continued, "he insisted we come see him every winter; he had a wonderful home with grapefruit, lemon, and orange trees all around. Everyday he'd take us—"

Dad grabbed the podium, a hand on each side, his head tilted slightly up, his eyes barely visible. To the casual observer, he could have been having a stroke.

Mom looked worried.

The ward Bishop made to get up, but the Presiding Bishop, a gnarled old gentleman with whom my father had grown up, grabbed his arm.

Then Dad was fine.

"When my brothers teased me, it was Lyle who—"

Dad crumpled in on himself, could have been a heart attack this time, and the Bishop actually made it to his feet before Dad, without looking back, froze him in place with a Jedi hand gesture. Stretching back to his full six-foot-two-inch height, no appearance of ailment this time; Dad looked skyward, as one receiving updates from on high. Then, clearly in possession of new programming, he leveled a now fiery gaze on the congregation; and Shirlene and I knew—Uncle Lyle's send-off was about to take a detour.

"You know," Dad began. "I hate to see discord and nastiness on the day we gather to honor Lyle's life—HATE IT!" reverberated through the chapel.

"Rancor seeps into the hearts, not only of the angry, but of everyone around—seeps—into the hearts and the minds of good people, tempting folks to laugh at pain, or take the Lord's name in vain, even at a family prayer, and it grrowwws!—It grows until soon, even the house of the LORD is rife with its stench—and we-will-not-have it!" Dads palm slapped the pulpit for emphasis. "Not on the day your father goes to his beloved bride."

"We'll adjourn to the gravesite shortly, where I would like you, Lydia, to again play that beautiful song. Collie will present a wonderful life sketch and YOU BOYS," Dad challenged. Eyes blazing, ears red, his finger pointed right at the family section.

"There's a little money—the girls get a little more. Those girls took care of your father when you couldn't be bothered. You know it's fair. You know it's right, and nowww—on this, his final day on earth, you will abide."

Meek nods responded and Dad was, well, Dad, again.

We marched en masse to the top of Cemetery Hill and laid Uncle Lyle to rest. My sisters and I hung back on the way down, watching Dad field funeral requests. It was only after the Relief Society dinner, when everyone was wrapping up, that my cousin's fiancé spoke up.

"Did your dad just call a family out *over money* in the middle of their father's funeral?"

We didn't even break stride. "Welcome to the family," Shirlene said.

THE PAINTED BUFFALO

Stephen Proskauer

Standing strong
On feathered legs
Towering Tetons
In his belly
Solemn prayers
In his heart

He blesses
White Buffalo Woman
With sacred smoke.
She bows to Earth
And gathers in
Its deep blue pain.

STARWAY

Tim Tarbet

IT WAS RAINING. IT WAS ALWAYS RAINING IN THIS DAMNED JUNGLE.

"Sergeant? Command is on the line. They want to talk to you."

A drip fell from a hole in the canvas above us.

I grumbled as I walked over to Corporal Wilkes. "How's the window?"

"Short. Only a couple more minutes before the tower moves."

"When's the next one?"

"Hours from now. They say it's urgent."

"What do they want?"

"They won't say, ma'am. They say it's for your ears only."

A drip splashed on the table, soaking my charts.

I sighed and shook my head. "Forward it to my drum."

"Roger," he said, typing away at the console. My earpiece chirped when he was done.

"This is Sergeant Yales. Receiving code five-o-four."

A voice crackled over the speaker. I put my hand to my ear, pushing the earpiece deeper.

"This is Major Hornwall. Dispatch code six-two-three."

"Confirming." I pulled the cipher out of my boot. It checked out. That or the League of Worlds had broken our codes. Again.

"Dispatch code confirmed. What have you got for me?"

"I'll be brief. Are you familiar with the starway at New Trent?"

I looked up. I could see it in the distance, a black monolith disappearing into the clouds.

"Yes sir. As far as I know, it's been disabled." Another drip.

"That has changed. League forces have entered the system. Forward elements are repairing it as we speak."

I grabbed the comm table to keep from falling.

"I believe you know what will happen if the League is allowed to repair that elevator."

"Yes sir."

"Good. Because it's going to be your job to take it out."

"What?! Sir, if the League's already dug in, I won't have the man-power to get in there, let alone the ordinance that I'd need to—"

"You're the only unit that's within striking distance and you've got two weavers. Figure it out."

The line went dead. Drip, drip, drip.

My hand fell away from my earpiece and joined the other on the table for support. Black crawled at the edge of my vision as I curled my fingers around the edges of the tabletop. How dare he? My hand was wrapped around the fat major's neck instead of the flimsy fold-out table, squeezing the life out of...

"Ma'am?"

I whipped my head around. The corporal's face was drained of color, sitting as far away from me as he could and still operate the comm. His hand was shaking, inching to his pistol. Standard issue 9mm caseless high velocity cartridge. Prone to failure after 3,200 shots. I looked down. The table had cracked where I gripped it and blood was filling the fissures.

"Find me Warrant Officer Jones."

"Yes, ma'am!" He ran down the hill to find Kat. Once he was gone I wiped the blood off my hands and tried to find the cuts in my skin. There weren't any. Blood dripped from the table.

My breath caught, my hands started shaking. I shook my head, clenched my fists, and forced myself to take several deep breaths. Drip, drip.

I turned away and sat on the dirt next to the comm and pulled out my belt knife, twirling it in my fingers. The comm tower whirred, moving to the next pre-programed position. Portable point to point laser communication was nearly impossible to track, and harder to intercept. Command says the best form of encryption is to not be heard, so we have fleets of the things peppered all over the planet. Not as effective as the quantum entanglement the League uses, but they've got a stranglehold on that technology.

Wilkes came back with my Warrant Officer, Katherine Jones, the only other female in my squad. I knew her from before this whole fiasco started. Before I knew I was a weaver. We went to school together. She was studying art, like I was.

I'll be damned if I didn't hug her half to death when she was assigned to my squad.

They both saluted when they approached, which I halfheartedly returned. "Thank you, Wilkes. Dismissed."

"Ma'am, regs clearly say that—"

"Dismissed, Corporal."

He glanced at Kat, who gave him a subtle nod. "We'll be fine, Corporal. Go."

He glanced at the blood pooling under the table, but retreated back down the hill to where the rest of the squad sat.

Kat sat on the dirt beside me. "Wilkes said you about lost it. What happened?"

I shook my head and scrubbed my forehead. "New orders, Kat. They're bad."

"They can't be worse than having us sit out here in the middle of nowhere for three months straight."

I took a deep breath. "They want us to blow up the starway."

She glanced at me out of the corner of her eye and laughed. A stray lock fell across her face. It was longer than it should have been, but I let it slide. She'd always had such pretty hair. Drip.

"Yeah, just as soon as they deliver the nuke," she said, the corners of her mouth curling up. She swept the strand back behind her ear.

"That's what we're for, Kat."

Her face fell, and she looked me in the eye. "You're not serious."

"Dead serious. Command says League ships are already in the system. They're repairing the starway as we speak."

Kat's mouth hung open. She looked at the ground, then back at me again. "What are we supposed to do about it?"

"We're the only strike force in range. If we can't take it out, our forces on this planet are done for."

Kat shook her head and rubbed her face, smearing grime across it. "So what's the plan?"

"We slip in fast and quiet. We beeline for the starway, blow the supports, then get the hell out of there in the confusion."

"Lexi, I'm not sure I can do something that big. I've only known that I'm a weaver for a few months. I can't even—"

"Hey," I put my hand on her shoulder and squeezed. "You can handle this. You're up to grade C weaves, a lot better than I was doing when I had your level of training, and I've got your back. Just follow my lead, and we'll get through this."

She pursed her lips, nodding slowly. She looked away and noticed the cracked table.

"Lexi," she said, "why is the table bleeding?"

We were just outside the city proper on Route 304. The place had been hit by an EMP when the fighting started, and the highway was littered with wrecked vehicles.

"I don't like it," said Kat. "It's too open. We should look for another way in."

I peeked over the hood of the vehicle we were hiding behind. No movement. It even looked like the rain was letting up. "It's the fastest way. We'll get to the starway before they even know we're here."

Kat shook her head. "I still don't like it."

"I'll lead out with a class 3F. If I sense anything, you just pop a 2C barrier."

"I'm not very good at defensive weaves, Lexi."

"You'll do fine." I patted her arm. "Lead them out, Warrant Officer."

I took a deep breath and closed my eyes while Kat signaled the rest of the squad. I slowly exhaled and let everything go. I let go of all sensation, all my cares, all my plans.

For a moment I simply was.

When I opened my eyes everything was made up of vibrating strands of light. The eggheads said the strands were the stuff that made up the universe. The fabric of reality, or something like that. Whatever they were, as weavers we could see them, strum them, tie them in pretty little knots. For the moment, though, I just observed them, watched the way they bent around my men. Sentient minds leave a dimple on reality, like ball bearings on a sheet of silk. I'd be able to sense the League forces before they saw us and either move around them or surprise them.

I don't know why it didn't work.

We had just passed the first set of buildings when they hit us. Johnson was dead before Kat was able to get her barrier up. It rippled as it absorbed the small arms fire, giving us just enough time to get to cover. I shouted orders to return fire, but then I looked over at Kat.

She'd taken cover behind an old civilian cargo truck, only couple of meters away from me. The thing looked like it was on its last legs before it had been riddled with bullets and heaven knows what else. She knitted her brow, concentrating. Hard. Way too hard. I yelled for her to drop her Weave, to let her barrier fall. She looked up at me in a daze, sweat streaking the dirt on her face. We locked eyes and blackness swam at the edges of my vision. Shouts became indistinct and the thud of gunfire little more than a pulse. Her pupils went wide.

Then she smiled.

She turned away, cocking her head as if she were hearing the gunfire for the first time. Her barrier fell as she stood and raised a hand toward one of the League soldiers and fried him with a lightning bolt. The blast knocked me on my ass, and I sat there, slackjawed. A class 1F directed energy attack. I hadn't taught her that. I wasn't sure I could do it myself. The gunfire stopped. Kat blasted two more by the time the League forces started diving for cover.

Gunfire split the air as the League troops tried to bring Kat down, but she swatted the bullets out of the air with her weaves, sending them spinning off in every direction. She cut down the ones who were smart enough to flee. She lashed out at some with more lightning bolts, her laughter splitting the air like nails on a chalkboard. Others simply exploded. Class 1G weaves. One of my men screamed; Private Aliyev was being dangled from his feet by a seven-meter tentacle. I don't think we even have a class for something like that. A clawed, dripping hand grabbed my ankle when I tried to run to him, sending me sprawling in the dirt. I yanked my pistol from its holster and sent three rounds into the dark under the vehicle I'd taken cover behind. Something in the darkness there squealed.

Kat always did have a very potent imagination. She walked through the battlefield, the eye of the hurricane. She danced to the tune of dying men's screams, destruction falling where she pointed, and nightmares following on her heels. I thought she was going to kill us all when a bullet tore through her shoulder.

She staggered back and looked around. A sandy-haired man, couldn't have been older than twenty, stood holding a heavy caliber pistol. A red Greek trident stood out on his shoulder. He fired again, guiding his shot with a weave. Kat grinned as the round bent around her and shattered a window. She closed the distance as he fired again and again, each shot bending around her to hit the vehicles behind her. When his pistol locked open he dropped it and ran at Kat. He jumped and snapped out a kick but she slipped out of the way. He hit the ground and rolled to his feet, weaving a machete into existence. The weave was sloppy; the blade wavered, and beads of sweat stood out on the man's forehead. He swung at her, lashing out again and again, but she just laughed, jumping out of his reach. The man growled. She'd toyed with the men at school this way, teasing them with her phone number. He roared, throwing all his weight behind his machete. Kat snapped her arm up and the machete hit her arm like a block of wood. She grinned as she drove her fist through his skull.

The headless corpse jerked and tumbled stiffly backwards, trailing crimson through the air. She held her hand up, watched the man's gore run down her arm. I glanced at my pistol. It seemed better, somehow. More personal than the rifles we use. I raised my weapon and aimed at the woman I'd known since college. She cocked her head, still smiling, and raised her arm in response. The machete was still lodged in it.

She was still smiling when I weaved a bullet between her eyes.

Kat's head snapped back with the impact, and she stumbled, trying to regain her balance. I don't know why I could hit her and the other guy couldn't. Maybe she was tired. Maybe she was so far gone that she didn't understand what was happening any more.

She probably just didn't expect her best friend to try to kill her.

I fired again, weaving this one into her chest. I fired again and again, tears blurring my vision. I forced each round to hit her ruined body. I emptied my mag into her before she finally hit to the ground.

I stood there a moment before my knees gave out, the last of my shots ringing in my ears. The rest of the battlefield was silent. I don't know how much time passed while I sat on the ground, my empty pistol smoking in my hands, tears streaming down my face. Shadows danced at the edge of my vision and the world seemed to darken. Black ink instead of blood spilled from Katherine's wounds and eerie creatures crawled out from under the cars to lap it up. The wind began to whisper things in my ear and...

"Ma'am?"

Wilkes tapped me on the shoulder. He was looking everywhere but at me. The other soldiers had taken up defensive positions around me, but they all stole glances at me and shuffled where they stood.

"Sergeant?" The corporal's voice cracked.

I shook my head and spat. My mouth tasted like blood. I looked over at Kat's body. She stared into the sky. Raindrops fell into her eyes and ran down her face. She looked like she was crying. I lurched to my feet and walked over to her. My pistol slipped from my trembling hands. My helmet joined it on the ground a moment later. I forced myself to kneel beside her. Her blood soaked my pant legs. Slowly I closed her eyelids, smoothed her hair. I tried to avoid looking at the gaping hole in her forehead. Slowly, I took her dog tags. The warm metal felt heavy in my hand. Tears blurred my vision and joined the rain. I closed my fist around Kat's tags, pressing it against my forehead, and quietly began to weep.

A timid voice came over my shoulder. "Ma'am I..." Wilkes swallowed. "Ma'm they could be coming back. We have to go."

Snot filled my nose, making me sniff. I nodded, scrubbing my eyes. He was right. I glanced up at him. "Grab the wounded. Secure the weapons from the men that Kat..." my voice caught in my throat. "That we killed. They should be better than ours."

He nodded once and strode off, relaying my orders. I watched him go. He looked back and opened his mouth then shook his head. I reached down to grab my pistol, but my hand stopped halfway. It was sitting in Kat's blood. My breath shuddered.

It was time for a new pistol anyway.

I rocked to my feet. What was left of my squad was waiting for me. All of them had one of the League's rifles except for Wilkes, who had two. Aliyev had an arm in a sling, and Smith was rocking back and forth, hugging himself. Jones, Durov, Ramius, and Johnson were missing. As I walked over to them I slipped Kat's dog tags into the pocket where I kept my other partners'.

LAETOLI, TANZANIA

Cynthia Loveland

More than three-and-a-half million years ago
she left her footprints in the ash,
fossilized, forgotten, found, and finally
studied with some kind of reliable science.

They think she bore the weight of a child on her hip—
while another…maybe two…trailed behind,
aping (but not apelike) her footfalls,
primitive and barely upright.

Kicking off from ancestors. Hobbling toward the future.

But they can't calculate how much her shoulders stooped
as she stepped through the stifling heat,
or how hard her lungs spasmed—trying to cough out ash,
fleeing punctuated equilibrium.

And they haven't yet hypothesized how many of her tears
joined the rain that made ash into mud—
the mud that preserved her heel-toe, heavy-hipped stride
as fodder for some article in *Nature* magazine.

After all the hours of observations—a plaster mold, a measurement—
and line after line of notes about half-life and bipedal locomotion,
she was just one more single mother
skirting the edge of disaster.

MY FATHER THE HORSE WHISPERER

Beth Moore

HOOVES THUNDERED ON THE HARD PACKED SOIL AS HORSES, manes and tails rippling in the wind, raced to where a man stood waiting. He had pushed open the big, creaking doors of the cavalry barn. The sound meant food.

As a little girl, sitting in the loft of the huge armory, I had never watched anything so grand, nor anyone as brave as my father, Charles Nephi Shumway, standing in the entrance of the stable. When those big horses reached him, they stopped. Most impatiently pawed the ground, stirring up dust clouds, but not one tried to go through the large doors until Dad stepped aside, as if giving permission.

Each one walked to his stall, paused a second, and looked at the name painted above his head, then pranced in and began to eat.

I know they can't read and so do you. Yet as a little girl I never doubted they could. Not many days passed, even in that little town, that someone didn't come to watch the horses *read*. Often, while they ate, visitors would stop to visit with my dad and listen to his tales. He loved to spin his stories almost as much as he loved his horses. His friends used to call him the *Will Rogers of the Big Horn Basin.*

His official title was Stable Sergeant in the National Guard. A full-time government job in depression days meant we always had a home and food. There's no such title today, I'm sure, because stable meant what it said. He was in charge of a stable that housed fifty to sixty feisty, big, dark-colored geldings—dark colored so they would be difficult to see in times of battle. He also trained the men and young boys how to take care of their assigned mount.

Dad had another man to help with feeding, watering, and grooming the horses, and he soon learned to do a good job or he did it over. Young men in the National Guard would often come to practice their riding, and give Dad a hand too. He always had time to listen as the young recruits would bend his ear with their problems or successes. They were *his* boys.

Often during the summer, in the cool of early evening before the sun set, the men and boys dressed in their uniforms and mounted their horses. The plaintive sound of the bugler had the company scrambling to get in formation for a parade. On special occasions the high school band led the way, and off they went to perform their drills in the big field next to the armory.

Again I watched from the loft, but at these events women and other kids kept me company. The smell of hay tickled our noses, and some of us chewed stalks which had a faint taste, matching how the hay smelled. Other odors of sweat, manure, and dust wafted up to us, but we didn't care. Even the busy mosquitoes having a feast was a minor nuisance.

The big doors in the loft where Dad pushed the hay out to the horses stood open, and I managed to get close to the edge for the best view. The distance to the ground frightened me, and Mom held tight to my arm. Chattering voices surrounded me, and I wondered why everyone didn't keep quiet and pay attention to the drill preparations. Didn't anyone else see the beauty in the movement of the horses as they tossed their big heads, and pawed the ground periodically in protest? The men and boys, *full of themselves,* sat ramrod straight in their saddles. But after the bugler, when the drum beat a cadence, and the other instruments filled in, everyone stopped talking, and we clapped enthusiastically in rhythm. This activity lasted until the inadequate lighting made it hard to see, children started fussing and thoughts of tomorrow's work day made the spectators start drifting away

After it was over my brothers went to help Dad, because he wouldn't leave until he made sure every horse had been properly watered and rubbed down by its rider.

Even with Mom by me, it seemed spooky at night when the people left. Constant cracks and moans filled the old tin barn as it cooled down. Otherwise active pigeons, who claimed the exposed beams in the unfinished ceiling for their home, had settled in for the night. Their droppings, a worry in daytime, ceased with dark. The movements of the horses, such fun to watch in the daytime, scared me at night with their restless sounds. A small breeze filled the air with the smell of manure—a strong smell that still, though it wrinkles my nose, brings back precious memories.

Finally Dad, my brothers, and the in-training soldiers were satisfied that all was well. Tired, but happy, everyone went home.

Troop A 115th Cavalry was one of the last in the United States to be disbanded. I like to think that it was because Dad cared so much about the horses in his charge. He won more awards than any other Stable Sergeant for the condition and behavior of his wards at the yearly summer National Guard Camps in Guernsey, Wyoming.

World War II ended the cavalry. What a sad day it was when Dad put *his* horses on the train. Ironically it was the same train that carried the National Guard with *his* boys on their way to war. Different destinations waited for them because the cavalry was outdated.

It wasn't only my father who had tears in his eyes. Many of the boys who watched the horses being loaded into the cattle cars, choked with emotion and wiped at their eyes when they thought no one was looking.

Although I didn't begin to understand how Dad must have felt, standing on the train platform, waving good-by to a loved way of life, I felt and shared his sadness. I stood close and slipped my hand in his. He squeezed it in acknowledgment, but kept his eyes fastened on *his* boys and their former mounts. Tears trickled down my cheeks as I remembered those happy times I'd watched Dad's horses read as they came in to eat. And how I'd thrilled seeing them drill in the field with their tails held high. Never would I forget the evenings in the hay loft watching the exciting maneuvers. Scenes that lived only in my memory as this part of my childhood were over. And now the reign of the Cavalry belonged to an honored place in history.

Efficient jeeps and tanks fill the roads in war time, but machines can't be a friend to their riders, nor thrill young and old hearts like horses did, with their uniformed soldiers marching in formation.

ANTELOPE CANYON

Marilyn Ball

Likely God saw the earth, a swirling mass,
turbulent and wild. Arms lifted, He reached
the whole, encasing all with passion peculiar,
placed it in the right confluence of the universe.
Each end of earth a trifle pointed, He said. The middle
greatness—equator.

Letting go, a step back, He decided to peel
earth's crust, tipped this sphere upside down,
tapped, thrust, serenely set it right: great pieces
of the shell fell away, deep cracks appeared
where birth of the southwest slot canyons
opened, were born.

Sequestered by high red stone walls, one serpentine
walkway through—He stepped along, saw the light
of pink-cream beauty, a sacred, golden glow
painting the huge up thrust walls.

Meandering past curves, juts of stone, He caressed
each a last time, felt the chilled, rough stones rest.
Using His fingers, sanded a rock in the shape of a heart,
then walked on—out into the sun…

DISAPPEARED

Andrea Hughes

RAIN STOOD ON THE LAWN NEAR THE EDGE OF THE CLIFF. She watched the paraglider soar off the grass of the Ritz Carlton. What would it feel like to fly like that, unbound by the earth? She had a fear of heights but was intrigued with the thought of sailing like a wind-blown leaf lifted by the breeze. She had been drifting around the country for a while now and kind of felt like a wind-blown leaf. Now she had landed in Laguna.

She had changed her name from Rain Song. Not too many people had a name like that. She wondered how her mother could ever have come up with that name. Her mom was kind of a hippy so that was probably the explanation. She really kind of liked her name but knew it was too unusual to use for a while. Her new name was Ashton, "Ashton Anderson the Blues Singer." She picked that name because she had spent part of her childhood in Ashton, Idaho, while her dad did dry-farming.

One thing Rain could do really well was sing. Her first job was at a bar in Green River, Wyoming. She knew how to sing the blues being well acquainted with the blues through different times in her life, the present being one of them.

The people in the bar usually liked her singing, and between what the bar owner gave her and her tips, she was able to make a meager existence for a while living at a cheap hotel. She didn't let people get to know her very well. She didn't want any attachments right now. All she wanted was freedom and safety.

Her next job was in Rapid City, South Dakota. That's where she started writing songs. The place she started singing, was called the "Blue Moon Café." She liked singing in the Café better than a bar because she didn't have to put up with obnoxious drunks trying to hit on her. The first song she wrote was called, "It's a Rainy, Rainy Day." She tried it out on the guests.

"Oh it's a rainy, rainy day at the Blue Moon Café
Things are lookin' gray since you went away
The juke box is singin' a sad old song,
*   and my heart's singin' right along*
The waitress keeps trying to make me smile,
*   but I just want to sit here and cry for a while*
'Cause it's a rainy, rainy day at the Blue Moon Café
*   things are lookin' gray...."*

Rain realized she was pretty good at writing songs about the blues, and people seemed to like the songs she wrote too. She put a few of them to music and found a recording studio in one of the small towns and created her own CD. It made her feel good to know she had created her own music.

The Midwest was kind of therapeutic for a while. The people were down to earth and friendly. She liked their solid, salt of the earth attitude. They were generous and had values, morals, and good Christian hearts. It was refreshing. She usually never stayed in any one place for more than a couple of months. She wasn't planning to put down any roots for a while. She kind of liked traveling around the country and getting the flavor of different towns and different states. Sometimes she wondered about her family and worried because she knew they were worrying about her, but she just couldn't risk surfacing right now. She knew her husband would find her and who knew if she would survive if he did.

Her husband had truly been a Jekyll and Hyde personality, silent and broody much of the time but then it was like living with a time bomb. If she ever tried to engage him in conversation, she never knew what would set him off. Suddenly he would blow up for no reason it seemed to Rain. He would break anything around him when that happened and if she was near him, he might lash out at her.

When he had her pinned on the bed with his fist looming above her and let it go right into the headboard making a hole in it, she knew the time had come to make an escape. She wondered how many other missing women were driven to run away and change identities to escape abuse. That night she snuck out the window and jumped off the roof. She ran past the tracks of the small Idaho town and on to the highway and started running and hitchhiking to anywhere anyone would take her.

◎ ◎ ◎

She wandered down the path to the beach from the Ritz Carlton. She had had an interview to be the singer at the lounge. She gave them her CD, but she didn't know if they were looking for her style of music. She had never worked in anything this up-scale before. She thought it might be an interesting adventure to meet a different kind of people. They wanted her social security number to apply for the job and that complicated things. Since she had been moving around, she'd always asked to be paid with cash and people didn't seem to mind but the Ritz Carlton was a legitimate place and things had to be done according to the rules and regulations.

When they called her a few days later and offered her the job, she decided to take it. She'd been moving around for about a year now. She wondered if it would be safe to start using her real name and decided to risk it. She had sent her family some letters without return addresses occasionally from different parts of the country but had never left a return address. The letters were brief telling them she loved and missed them and that she was okay but needed some time alone right now to find herself and what she really needed out of life. She told them that if her husband inquired about her, they didn't know where she was. It was true, they didn't. She asked them to please not have anyone come searching for her. She would get in contact with them when she was ready.

Rain liked it here in Laguna because it was by the ocean. She had always wished to live near the ocean. Growing up, her father took her and the family down to California every few years to see some relatives. The first time she saw the ocean she was captivated. She loved the smells, the feel of the sand, the sea shells, the seagulls, the salty damp spray, and the sea breezes carrying messages through the wind of other places, other people, and other times. Maybe it was her name, but Rain loved to be around any kind of water. She loved lakes, streams, rivers, ponds, and of course the rain. There was something mighty and fierce yet tranquil and calming about water.

There was something about Laguna that held her in its spell. The cliffs and the water had almost a mystical feeling when she was at the water's edge. Maybe she would settle down here for a while. This was the first place she had felt like might be home. She could never get enough of beach combing or just watching the waves roll in and out. She liked to bring her notebook down to the beach and write songs or poetry. The beach and water felt very healing to her. One day she wrote,

> Oh Sea, take me away with you to another place,
>   another time
> Reach out with your great arms and hold me
> As your tide draws back into itself take my bruised heart
>   with you
> Take away the loneliness, the heartache, the grief,
>   I have heaped up inside my self
> You have been my friend, my companion,
>   and my great healer so often
> Once again I come to you
> Caress me with your motion,
> Soothe me with your pounding surf
> Wash me clean again.

Sometimes when Rain was sitting and watching the waves, she would see a young man walking on the rocks out at the edge of the shore. He had lots of black, curly hair and wore a green khaki jacket and denim pants that had a few holes in them. He was usually bare foot. He would look out at the ocean and stare at it for long periods. Sometimes he would sit on the rocks close to the edge of the water and the waves would crash up around him. Rain felt a kindred connection to him. He seemed to be a loner like her but was drawn to the sea like she was.

One day Rain was walking along the edge of the water staring down at the little gifts the waves left behind. She looked up just as someone was passing. It was the young man on the rocks. Their eyes met and a strange but strong feeling came over her. His eyes were a deep aquamarine and drew her in like a magnet. She had never seen eyes like that before. He nodded and gave her a faint smile as he passed.

After that Rain noticed whenever she was at the water, he was often there too. She felt strangely drawn to him and didn't really understand why. One day she decided to venture out on the rocks where he often was to explore things from his vantage point. There were little tide pools with sea life living in them. There were different colors of anemones and sea cucumbers in their own little biome. She sat down to study them more closely. Suddenly a shadow covered her, and she looked up to see the young man standing behind her.

"Do you see anything interesting today?" he asked.

"These tide pools are really full of life aren't they."

"Yes, it's interesting how everything interacts with everything else."

"So many interesting colors and shapes too," said Rain. "I like the sounds of the water here too. They can be calm yet fierce at the same time."

The young man was quiet and looked out across the water as he often did.

"Have a nice day," he said as he began working his way out further to the edge of the rocks.

As Rain got to know the Laguna beaches, she became familiar with some sea caves along the shore. People could wander into them but had to be careful of the tides and only go at certain times so they didn't get trapped. She found a kind of fern and reed grotto and noticed it looked like someone had a makeshift hut that was kind of hidden. There were a lot of homeless people that made their living somehow on the beaches of California. The beach patrol tried to control it but they had their secret ways of surviving. She wondered if that young man she saw alone all the time was one of them.

The patrons that came to the lounge at the Ritz Carlton were a different kind of people. They were more impersonal. They were well dressed and sophisticated. They met other men and other women to discuss business and pleasure. They rarely acknowledged Rain. She was just kind of the background music. It made her feel even more isolated and alone because they were so indifferent to her. She had rented a small one bedroom studio in the center part of Laguna. What she made at the Ritz barely covered her rent and overhead, but somehow she squeaked by. Living by the ocean made it all worth it.

One day she was walking around the sea caves and ran into the strange young man again walking the other way. He gave her a nod and a faint smile and she smiled back.

"Good morning," he said.

"Good morning," she smiled.

"Great Day isn't it!"

"Yes, it's a beautiful today," she agreed.

He turned and started walking with her.

"Mind if I join you on your walk?"

"No, please do, I could use some company."

"Would you like to see one of my favorite spots for sea watching?"

"Sure," she said. She instinctively knew he was a safe and gentle soul. She had watched him enough to know this about him.

She followed him up to a gentle sloping cliff. There was a slight path through strategic places to reach the top. When they reached the top, the view was breath taking. The sea could be viewed for a hundred and eighty degrees. Sea gulls were catching wind currents, diving and soaring and calling to each other.

They sat quietly at the top of the cliff watching the birds.

Conversation didn't seem needed between them as they enjoyed the beauty of the place.

Finally he looked at her, his eyes drawing her in.

"Where do you come from?" he smiled. I know you're not a local because I pretty much know all the locals."

Rain's eyes looked sad and faraway. She didn't answer.

"Sorry, I didn't mean to pry. It doesn't really matter. You're here now and that's all that matters."

She smiled, "Yes, this place seems more like a home than most places I've been."

"The ocean seems like home to me too," he said. I'm never quite as content and happy as I am here. There's a certain kind of companionship I feel here with the sea life, the waves, and the birds. They sat again in silence listening to the sea sounds and the gulls around them.

"You know what? I've seen you a lot, but I don't even know your name. I'm Sky and you're?"

She laughed, "You're not going to believe this, I'm Rain,"

He smiled, "Actually that works. Not fire and rain, but Sky and Rain. It makes a good combination. We create clouds." They both laughed.

"I like clouds a lot too. I can always see different things in them. I notice angels a lot in clouds."

Sky smiled again, "I know another secret place that not too many people know about. Would you like to see it?"

"Okay, if it is as good as this place, I've got to see it."

They climbed back down and walked the beach for a while. They spotted some sea lions playing on some rocks and then a group of dolphins spinning through the air and playing in the ocean. Little

Sand Pipers were playing tag with the waves.

"The Sand Pipers are some of my favorite. They know just when to walk to the edge of the water and when to hurry back as the wave comes in. They are so amusing."

"They are funny little birds," Sky agreed.

Then a steep cliff towered over the sand.

"This is it." Sky pointed to the top.

"Wow, that's pretty high," Rain said nervously.

It was a more difficult climb up. Sky reached down to help Rain climb a steeper part of the incline. She felt a warmth and tenderness, yet strength as he grabbed her hand.

When they reached the top of the cliff, Sky stood at the edge and opened his arms. "Isn't it magnificent!" Rain stood back from the edge. Her legs felt like jelly. "Please come back a little, you're making me nervous." He stepped back.

"I'm feeling a little queasy. It's beautiful but I don't like to be right at the edge of cliffs. I'm not sure if it is a fear of heights or a fear of falling. Actually I have had rapture of the heights before and felt like jumping. Have you ever felt that?"

"No, I've never felt that, but I could see why you would feel uneasy around the edge."

He smiled and took her hand. "Are you okay?" She nodded. "Come with me, there's still more to see." They climbed down on the other side of the cliff and there was a quiet enclosed beach between sharp cliffs. The cliffs almost made a circle around the beach and there was a narrow slit between the rocks out to the ocean. In the middle of the sand was a deep blue pool.

"We're here just at the right time. When the tide comes up, we can't be in here because it is dangerous." He walked to the pool, dropped his clothes, and dove in.

Rain was a little shocked when he did that.

"Come on in!" he shouted. "It's a natural hot spring and the perfect temperature."

His freedom and exuberance and the natural elements of the

place made her want to join him, but she was a bit shy.

"Come on," he said. "I'll turn my back if you want."

Rain giggled shyly but decided to join him. Everything felt so natural and right in this hidden place.

"Okay, turn your back." He turned his back and she took off her light shift and slid into the water. It was the perfect temperature, not too hot and not too cold.

She was amazed that she could be so free, but it felt so natural and beautiful. It just felt like the right thing to do. They both swam and dove under the water playing and enjoying the water. Then she realized that they didn't even have towels and wondered how they would dry off.

Sky walked out on the beach and lay down on the sand on his stomach. Rain decided to follow him. They both laid there together and felt the sand and sun warming their backs and drying them.

After a while Sky said, "It's so perfect here. I hate to leave, but the tide is coming in so we better get going; it's dangerous if we don't. You can dress first. I'll keep my eyes closed." He smiled and closed his eyes.

Rain laughed and started dressing then walked towards the ocean. Sky joined her a few minutes later. "We can't risk staying here any longer. Come on." The waves were already licking the rocks around where they stood.

"This place is amazing. We have definitely got to come back here again," Rain said.

"We will," Sky agreed.

She didn't see Sky at the beach for a few days after that, and she wondered where he had disappeared. She watched the waves curl and crash and wondered what it would be like to be a sea creature and live in the water all the time. She imagined and longed for it sometimes. She often felt that she must have come from the sea. She felt like she was an amphibian and had to spend at least some of her time by the water each day. Rain was a Pisces and thought her astrological sign fit her well. She wrote a poem called "Pisces" that day.

Pisces
I am drowning of air
Suffocating from the sun's fire
Cast on the beach
Wounded
Weak
Gasping for water
Aching for death
Yet clinging to life
Throw me back to that cool deep abyss
Where my heart can breathe
And my soul can
Exist

Just as she finished writing, she saw Sky walking towards her. The sun was in her eyes so she brought her hand up to cover them.

"Hi, where have you been? I haven't seen you for a few days."

"Oh, sometimes I go out on a fishing charter and help with the fishing."

"Oh," Rain answered. That kind of explained how he might be making a living. Rain had wondered about that.

"What are you writing?" He sat down next to her. They really didn't know much about each other except that they were both beach hounds.

"I just wrote a poem. I like to write down by the water."

"Would you mind sharing it?"

"Okay," Rain felt comfortable sharing her poetry with him. He felt like a soul friend.

After she read it to him he said, "I relate to that poem. I'm a sea dweller at heart"

She didn't see him again for a few more days and then he mysteriously appeared again.

"There you are," Rain said. "I miss you around here when I don't see you."

"I miss it too. Do you feel like going to the secret hot spring again?"

"Yes!" I've been thinking about it and how wonderful it was a lot."

"Can you go right now?" Sky asked

"Yes, I don't have to work until tonight."

"Let's go then."

"Sounds good."

When they reached the pool inside the cliffs he said, "Come here. There's something else I want to show you. We didn't have time the other day."

They wandered back towards the back of the cliff. There was a crack between the rocks.

"This is an amazing sea cave. You won't believe it."

"What about light? Don't we need flash lights?"

"No, you'll see,"

When they entered the cave, it was already kind of lit up.

"Where is the light coming from?" Rain asked.

"Luminescent rocks."

"That's incredible." Rain said in amazement. As they wandered further into the cave, it became more and more fascinating. Large crystals were growing in different parts of the cave. The luminescent rocks glowed in different colors. There was a powerful mystical feel to the cave. There were some dripping sounds, and it became darker as they went further into the cave. Sky took her hand to help her along. Rain wondered how far they had come.

"We should probably go back now. I'm not sure what the tide is doing. It's easy to lose track of time in here. It really draws you in."

They started heading back and it seemed like a long time before Rain saw a crack of light ahead. She could hear the ocean waves crashing around the entrance of the cave.

"We've got to hurry." Sky was almost dragging her now through the cave trying to get to the entrance.

When they reached the mouth of the cave, water was crashing all around it. The tide was rapidly coming in.

"We're going to have to swim and swim hard so we don't get dragged out by the undertow,"

Rain looked at Sky with frightened eyes as they dove into the water. They were swimming hard but could not fight the incoming waves or the undertow. It was taking them steadily out to sea. Rain was becoming exhausted. Sky tried to swim and carry her like a life guard would, but the waves were too powerful. After fighting the waves for several hours, Sky looked at Rain. They couldn't fight any longer and they both knew it.

"Are you ready to join the sea?" He looked deeply into Rain's eyes.

Rain looked into his eyes and nodded.

"When you go under, take a big breath and you will become a sea creature," he smiled.

He grabbed her hand. They both closed their eyes and dove beneath the surface.

FOURTEEN DAYS OF RAIN

Isaac Timm

College of the Redwoods,
huddled under a balcony, I drag off my cigarette,
watch a flock of robins hop in the rain
as I dream of a frozen December
when I held you near the window and saw the moon reflected
on an icy parking lot.

I flip the butt. It sails into a bucket
like a downed biplane.
A robin makes a sound of crackling paper
as it shakes water from its feathers.

This relationship happened too fast. You said
As you peeked around the door frame and told me
I couldn't come in. First exile.

Then second, kicked from my house
I stared at the asphalt of a Cedar City convenience store
waiting for the Greyhound to take me to Eureka,
the bench paint cracked and dust rolled in from Milford.

I rolled north to Salt Lake City and then to Oakland,
pressed to the window by a fat man,
who barked about the rambling ranch house
he'd buy in Carson City.

The robins that flew by, ones and twos, to the coast
before the snow, now flock across the quad
in their stilted, jerky movements.
Before today, I'd never seen more than one.
Now they troop like red flags under the fog.

All week I've been flirting with a married woman.
She stuck her tongue out.
I told her, *That's only polite if you share.*
But she called my bluff, whispered in my ear
Where is a safe place we can go?
I stammered, my cool done blown.
I could think only of you. She smirked, disappeared,
damp cloth clinging to her shoulders as she faded in the rain.

A robin gives regard with bean-black eyes,
tears a worm in two.

MATCHING BAGGAGE

Timothy James

You don't really get a say in where you're from. Whether by destiny or twist of fate, the decision is made for you. Some people get Taos, Tahoe, or Malibu; still others, New York, San Francisco, or Key West.

Me? I got the hindermost corner of Idaho. Could have been worse, I suppose. My parents are from places Google Earth couldn't find with all the satellites in orbit. Places with deserted main streets, rotting bandstand skeletons, and very little hope. Dad grew up in the mountain ranching community of Mink Creek, named for a creek and the small fur-bearing animal that once prowled its banks. Some imagination those pioneers had—criminals actually, not the bad kind, though. Mink Creek served as a hiding settlement for Mormon polygamists on the run from federal agents.

Mother cut her teeth in the ever-so-slightly more cosmopolitan dust bowl of Winder before moving—here, lucky her. Oh, it's a decent enough place; I see that now. But there was a time in the not so distant past, when I couldn't wait to get out. I didn't care what I had to do. I didn't care if I starved, and I very nearly did.

My determination paid off though. By age twenty-eight I had clawed my way into a junior partnership at M.H.I. While my alter ego, Tommy Connelly, had just cracked the best seller list. Which my friends decreed, was cause for celebratory drinks at Tacky's.

The next thing I remembered was the claxon of my phone at the obnoxious hour of nine o'clock on a Saturday morning. "Hello," I rasped, watching a very nice set of newly-familiar glutes re-pack a ripped pair of Calvins.

"Tad? You sound awful! Are you coming down with something?"

"Hi, Mom," I said as my new friend waved goodbye.

I'd barely noticed another week had gone by, until "the call," that is. See, I rarely called home. Not that I disliked my family or anything, quite the opposite. It's just that calls from home, reminded me of, well—home, and the person I used to be.

When I call, I can't get off the phone. If I wait, Mom calls me and we're done in five minutes. Mom is from a time when making a long-distance phone call was something to be considered with great care, like the purchase of furniture or a car. Once made, the call follows a model of military efficiency: say only what you must, prod them to do the same, hang up as quickly as possible, then pour over every scrap of information like a cryptographer.

We were only two minutes in, but already the call felt long. I was sort of itching to end the thing, but Mom showed none of the usual signs of wrapping up.

She delivered the news with a deceptively casual air, right after the weather, and speculation on the reproductive status of the family cat.

"Grandma has cancer," she said. Followed by words like "inoperable" and talk of timeframes generally reserved for perishable foods, or a book on loan from the library.

Grandma—my buddy, my cross-country training partner, my cheering section for wrestling—she can't be sick, not really.

"It's spread to her liver. She's decided not to fight it."

"What? Why the hell not?"

"She wants to enjoy what time she has," Mom soothed, "to stay in her home, and have her family around her."

I saw where this was going, of course I did. A glance at the clock was enough to confirm my suspicions. Mom, now well into our seventh minute, showed none of the usual signs of slowing down.

"It won't be long before she'll need help for everything," she said. "The family will have to step up, but Cal and Bruce have families of their own. Mel lives in Salt Lake, and Shauna will do what she can, but between school and the kids—"

And so on, with the various excuses for my siblings—my hetero-sexual siblings–whose lives were simply too important to interrupt.

"All of a sudden it's great that I'm gay," I mused. *"Only took you 12 years!"*

The distant hiss of long distance static snapped me back to reality. Nine minutes and counting, nine minutes and there was static, honest to God silence on the still-open line.

"Can you come?" she whispered.

My mind flashed back 10 years, to the last time I saw her. I was loading my pickup when she called. Mom took the message. "Grandma wants you to stop by your way out."

"Great," I muttered under my breath, "another last minute pep talk."

◉ ◉ ◉

Grandma is waiting in the enclosed porch, when I arrive, and ushers me inside for a "quick snack." Her house smells like fresh baked bread.

My mouth waters as she disappears into the kitchen.

She returns with a butter and sugar slathered slice and settles into her recliner while I eat.

"All set?" she asks.

"Yes, Ma'am."

"You'll call?"

I nod, surreptitiously checking my watch.

"We have colleges here, you know."

"Grandma!"

"I know, I know. You have to be out in the world, always did, even when you were a little boy, always exploring, trying new things."

If I don't cut this short, I may as well not go today at all.

"I love you, Grandma," I say, but of course it doesn't work.

"I love you too, dear. Now have a seat—or are you in too big a hurry for your old grandmother?"

I sigh and park on her giant, pink sofa. Ten minutes or all day, I'm here until she's done. I love these chats; always have, ever since

I was a kid. But today I answer politely and nod in all the right places. Before long, she pushes out of her recliner with a grimace.

Age is finally catching up with her. I push the thought away before it can be true.

"All right," she says, "since you're in such an all-fired hurry. I have something for you, though."

She hands me a small box wrapped in that shiny chrome and lavender wrapping paper, the stuff people use when no theme really matches the occasion.

"Open it."

My finger slides carefully along the taped seams; it wouldn't do to appear rushed. As the paper unfolds, a shirtless Adonis, and the words "Trojan" and "Pleasure Pack" appear.

"I hope you find what you're looking for," she says. "Just be careful, so you don't catch AIDS."

Tears well up in my eyes and suddenly I'm flying into her arms. I wanted to come out to her years ago, but Mom and Dad warned it would break her heart.

"How'd you know?"

Grandma actually cackles. "You have to get up pretty early in the morning to fool this old girl. They're the ribbed kind," she adds conspiratorially. "They're supposed to feel better."

I don't have the heart to tell her they're the sexual equivalent of a rumble strip.

I should have trusted her. Hell, I should have told her first.

◎ ◎ ◎

I looked around my Las Olas Boulevard loft at the evidence of the life I'd built. Tastefully erotic art on the walls, custom kitchen, the Bang and Olufson home theater, and Recaro furniture. Could I come? Of course I could—would. I found myself wondering two things: how much would all this fetch at the yard sale? And what the hell was I going to do in Idaho?

◎ ◎ ◎

The one thing I swore I'd never do. I drove the length and the breadth of the United States once more. North along the Atlantic, then west through the deep oppressive heat of the Bible Belt. North again, and west across the sun-baked grasslands of Kansas and Oklahoma. There I entered that uneasy daze, born of the exhaustion, that comes not only with the strain of travel, but the knowledge of how far there is to go.

On the far side of the vast high deserts of Colorado and Wyoming, I reached the home stretch. Around Bear Lake, through a mountain pass and voilà, 3 days and 2,537 miles from civilization, I rolled into my home town. *Only 9:00 and already the place is deserted.*

I thought about home, *my* home. The city would just now be coming to life. Happy hour at the Marlin as the waves lapped the beach, go-go boys at Tacky's, maybe even a show at Shangri-La.

Still, the lure of the past was stronger than I'd anticipated. Trials and pains, once all-consuming seemed barely to register; victories, even the smallest, called like a siren's song, and I couldn't resist a bit of exploration for old times' sake. We had a Subway now; could additional perks of civilization be far behind? A McDonald's perhaps, maybe even a Wal-Mart!

Eventually, I drove by "Hillbilly High" a stifling, industrial, edifice, once the bane of my existence; now, it was as if the whole thing had shrunk. Just a building, a dead or dying reminder of a boy, insecure, the one who ran away. It was hard to believe I'd ever roamed the halls of this place, harder still to believe I was back.

The clock on my car radio read 9:47; the folks would be worried. I put the car in gear and drove toward my childhood home.

Goodbye Sunday brunch and mimosas by the pool. Goodbye theater and art and Christmas on the beach. Goodbye job where my name was preceded by mister, and loft overlooking the Intercostal. Hello—home.

A mere two-hour drive from the nearest city and at least a dozen light years from the 21st century. Home of fry sauce, rodeos and Christmas lights.

Mom greeted me at the door like the prodigal son returned, not bad for folks whose sleeping habits follow the sun.

It was late summer on the ranch, so when I wasn't helping with Grandma, I hauled hay, moved sprinkler pipes, and chased cows. I found the ease with which I'd settled back into rural life bothersome. Even more so, the realization that time had now become my enemy. It always was of course, but now it had attitude. Grandma's illness and the fact that my parents had somehow gotten old, served to remind me of my own mortality. Alone and bored I was, keenly aware of the seconds ticking irretrievably by.

To make matters worse, people constantly approached me, ostensibly to chat, but angling hard for even the tiniest bit of gossip. They'd close with, "if there's anything we can do," like they'd really be interested in bedpans or morphine. I reminded myself that soon I'd be gone—then reeled with the guilt of wanting to be.

Simple errands like a trip to the store became a game, a reconnaissance mission—avoid all contact, get the stuff and return. One day at the pharmacy, my flesh tingled at the sound of an all-too familiar voice, and there he was: Tony Blakely. His head, anyway, floating between the shelves of laxatives and prophylactics, like the ghost of dramas past. I should have said hello, but our time together was over. Except, there he was, and here I was—again. Which thought spurred me into evasive action. I heard his call in the distance as my car door closed. *Not as clean as I'd have liked, but mission accomplished.* He disappeared back into the store like a phantom.

Grandma, meanwhile, as she'd done her whole life, took pride in beating her doctor's dire predictions. Slipping, yes, almost by the day, but spry. She reveled in visits from friends and family, some not seen in years. Determined to leave this world in an orderly fashion, she took to leaving post-it instructions around the house, recording the family history and secret recipes for posterity. The mere admiration of any object, regardless of size or value, was all it took to turn her into a geriatric game show hostess.

Only she noticed my malaise.

"You should call on old friends," she suggested.

"Maybe."

"Tammy asked after you at church."

Grandma had served in the LDS Primary for five decades, and anyone she'd taught, regardless of age or disposition would to her, forever have the childhood "y" attached their name. Timmy, Johnny, Taddy and Tammy—Tamara, formerly Jameson now Blakely, married to the before mentioned Tony.

Tamara had long since morphed from childhood innocence into one of the nastiest people it had ever been my displeasure to know. She enjoyed a brief stint as a small-time pageant queen, which celebrity, however limited, earned her a pass from most who didn't know her.

"She's not my friend, Grandma," I said.

"Well Anthony certainly is; they said you should drop by for a visit."

Suddenly I was sixteen all over again. Before I could catch myself, the words "Tony said that?" betrayed my worldly facade.

I think everyone has a Tony in their past, that one impossibly cool friend, so beautiful it hurts. That shock of thick hair that always did what it wanted. The girls clung to him like flies on shit—even the guys were in love with him.

Grandma smiled. "He was with Tammy when she asked, said you should drop by this—oh my goodness! Is it Friday already? You'd better get going."

A trap

"Nah," I said. "I'd rather hang out with you."

"Did I forget to tell you? Linda's coming by to do some quilting tonight. My memory's getting so bad these days."

"There's nothing wrong with your memory, Grandma."

"Must be the cancer," she said managing a cough or two for effect.

"Liver cancer, Grandma, *not* lung."

"There, you see? Go see your friend," she said.

67

It was late in the afternoon, the sunset scorching the tops of the pine trees that lined the outskirts of town. I drove past the house twice before I realized it was the right one. Tall weeds surrounded an oasis of civility, a large, well-manicured lawn led to a flower garden which circled the house, broken only by an enclosed porch. An intrepid, young Big Wheel pilot skidded to a sidelong stop, as I walked up the drive. "Hey there," I said. "Is this the Blakely's?"

A head popped up from the shadow of the porch; "Who's there?" she asked.

I recognized her at once.

"Hello Tamara," I said.

"Tad Benson! Tony said you were in town. How you been? We missed you at the last reunion," she continued. "How's your grandma? I seen her at church, but you know how she is, wouldn't call the fire department if her front porch went up in flames. Tony! Come look who's here."

My participation in the conversation didn't seem necessary, and at that moment the young Big Wheeler broke for the open road. I laughed as Tamara took off in hot pursuit yelling, "Ethan Anthony Blakely! You get yer skinny butt back here!"

"Tad Benson, back again," Tony said from the door. "So are you just here to help with your grandma or thinking of staying on?"

He looked exactly the same! Okay, well, not exactly the same—better. The jawline was stronger, the cheeks more defined. He'd put on a few pounds, but his stomach was still flat and that reckless shock of hair still stubborn. The body beneath the white shorts and dopey Def Leopard T-shirt had solidified into something worthy of being showcased in marble.

He clapped his hand on my shoulder. "Dude, say something."

"Umm yeah—hi," I said, my chest so tight I could barely speak.

Tony pulled me through the entryway into the kitchen and didn't let go until he'd sat me down at the table. I couldn't believe how good the years had been to him. They certainly hadn't done Tamara any favors. Three kids had undone her beauty-queen figure, though motherhood seemed to have mollified her personality deficiencies.

"Ten years, and you look exactly like you did the last time I saw you," Tony said.

I glanced down at his wedding band, wondering if he was really thinking of the last time we were together.

"You too," I mumbled.

"Liar!" He laughed.

"Only thing missing's a skateboard."

"Well—I don't do much boarding anymore," he said.

"Too bad," I mumbled.

"Excuse me?"

"The skateboard," I said. "It's too bad you don't ride anymore."

"Wanna pop?" Tony asked, getting up from the table. He didn't wait for my response, just looked surreptitiously around the corner, and got us two Cokes from the fridge.

"Actually," he half whispered as he slid passed me to sit down, "I do sometimes. Don't tell Tamara though; she hates it."

I had to laugh. "Not so bad as secrets go."

Tony smiled, "So what about you?"

"What about me?"

"Tell me your secrets, son!"

"No secrets here," I said.

Undaunted, he dove right into old times.

"Hey, remember that old trailer down the hollow? Dude! Best porn stash ever."

"Ever?" I asked. "You have at least heard of the internet right?"

"And the time we snuck that *Penthouse* up to scout camp," Tony continued. "Micksel was so pissed, he made us watch while he burned it."

"Didn't stop him from giving each page a long, creepy look," I said.

"Hey remember that centerfold? I mean, damn!"

"Not really, no."

"For real? You gotta remember those perfect tits."

What, is he kidding me with this shit?

"It wasn't the centerfold I was looking at."

Tony grinned. "Me either," he said, and then his foot was in my crotch.

"Are you out of your fucking mind?"

Tamara stepped in from the yard. "Language, guys," She said. "We have kids in this house."

"Yeah, Tad." He chuckled. "Watch your language."

"Uh, sorry," I said to her back as she bustled through the living room. I couldn't remember the last time I had to watch my language.

A young girl ran through the kitchen calling, "Daddy, can I watch TV?"

He began kneading me with his foot. "Sure, sweetie."

"Jeez, Tone," I hissed, "your kid!"

Tony laughed. "Uncle Taddy's funny, huh Sweet Pea?"

"Uh huh," she said.

"It's *Aladdin*," he explained. "Nothing's gonna distract her from *Aladdin*."

"I'm off to book club," Tamara announced, coming back through the kitchen. "The kids have a play date at the Peterson's at seven, but Connie said you can send them over anytime. The boys are outside and Miley's watching TV, so be sure you drop them off before you go anywhere."

"Just drop 'em on your way, will you Hon?"

"Tony! I'm late."

"Please? I'll get Tommy here to sign your book for you if you do," he coaxed, foot still working.

"Oh I'm sorry," she said. "Do you go by Tommy now?"

"S'ok," I managed, "it's just a pen name."

"Well what ever you want to be called, I just love it!"

"I hope you remember us when you're rich and famous," Tony said.

"What makes you think I'm not?" I said, my poker face stretching that last royalty check to the limit.

Tony responded with "the face," a lopsided grin that'd been getting him out of trouble since we were kids, and of course Tamara melted—just like *I* used to.

Everyone gets their share of socially awkward moments in life. Though I dare say that having signed my pen name to a trashy teen romance novel, for an old acquaintance, while getting a foot job under the table from her husband in the inattentive presence of their kid—not to mention the doing of it in a calm and affable manner—has earned me a free ride in the next life, regardless of what else happens in this one.

Even so, the moment her car left the garage, I brushed his foot away and got up to leave.

"Kept track of you over the years," he said. "Funny thing about that internet, spell a guy's name just a little differently on a web search and…well, it kind of reminded me a lot of the stuff you and me and Gabe got into."

I froze, just for a second, but long enough to widen his grin.

"I'm not ashamed," I snapped. "I got out; I did what I had to do. *I* made it, and if you think for one second—"

"You were right," he said.

"What?—Right about what?"

"About a lot of things."

I forced myself to calm. I *had* gotten out, I could do so again; his was a life sentence.

"Look," I said. "I just want to make sure the lines don't get crossed here."

"They've been crossed before," he said.

"Dude, we were what, sixteen? You're married!"

"Seventeen—and I was beginning to think you'd forgotten."

"I remember everything."

"So that line you mentioned, what if we crossed it? What if I were to touch like this?" His hand headed south as his lips brushed mine.

"Jesus."

"Tell me you don't want to."

"So what if I do?" I whispered. "What about your kids, your wife? They mean anything to you?"

"They mean everything to me."

"Where does that leave us?"

"You mean everything too."

"Tony! You can't have it both ways."

"So that's it then? One mistake and I'm done?"

"I didn't say that!"

"Dude, she's not you okay? I'm dyin' here. When I saw you were back, I mean we were good together, right? I know I've got baggage, I just thought, maybe, if we were careful—" his voice trailed off.

Everything around me melted away—the crappy JC Penney kitchen, the clapboard house, the whole hideous little town. Had I slid so far down the moral ladder that wedding vows held no meaning?

◉ ◉ ◉

On a cold November day the week before Thanksgiving, Grandma died. That the sun still rose seemed incredibly unjust. Tony stayed close during service, at the cemetery, and through the Relief Society dinner. We were cleaning up when he pulled me close, nuzzling my ear. I fell into his embrace. It felt right, like I'd finally made it home.

"I should go," he whispered. "Tammy and the kids will be worried. You gonna be okay?"

I nodded.

"Vegas next weekend?"

I smiled. Like grandma said: "We all have baggage; the trick is getting it to match."

EQUILIBRIUM

Cynthia Loveland

The first rule of thermodynamics
no one bothers with much,
but the second says warm flows to cold,
which explains how and why

romances end the way they do,
in apathy or anger directly
proportional to passion.
All that heat flows somewhere else
to kindle another dying spark.

Maybe we could be happy
if we didn't have such...uh...short

      attention.

          spans.

But we are a sound-bite in perpetuity,
a testament to the impermanence of
things that don't run backwards because we want them to,
of chocolate milk that won't unstir itself,

or shattered cups that don't jump back
onto the table reassembled just because
we wished they hadn't fallen when they fell.
Instead, we slice our heels on Time's Arrow,

mop up the floor with Kleenex-brand entropy
and stitch the lacerated layers
      back
             together.

LOVING WORDS MADE HER CRAZY

Carroll Shreeve

LEXIE LOVED WORDS, ESPECIALLY THE ONES MEANT TO SEDUCE her. Too innocent, it took her longer than most women to figure out she was a fool for drool due to do her love-starved past. Telegraphing without wires, love-need was her pheromone scent. Men obeyed it.

Routinely falling for the wrong guy and sticking up for him—and with him—beyond all common sense drove her to the refrigerator. Falling in and out of love, breaking hearts, including her own, turned her into some kind of serial killer. Or was it cereal in a box? If she got all the way to the bottom of it, which happened with crunchy regularity, would she figure herself out?

Men's patterns, her patterns became too familiar to be amusing. When one laughed through his third gin and tonic, with each sip their relationship ebbed away as if he had an eraser and didn't care where he used it. Much to her dismay, his habit helped *him* forget— even the ever-so pretty, powerful words he used to seduce her.

Lexie tried to medicate the fearful stomach flutters with food like he did with cocktails. Numbing with snacks didn't erase the pain and humiliation or the shame.

Later, when she'd have to walk away from his cavalier attitude, he'd be crushed and blame her for betraying him. She was as addicted to him, to food, and to drama as he was to his gin. It made her feel and act crazy.

Betrayed by words with different meanings to her than to another man who'd ensnared her with tender, promising words, she fell again. She'd sucked up enticing words of lasting joys to come. Those that meant most to her he denied saying. Such words slipped deliciously off the man-of-the-moment's tongue and took a direct route to her heart or her brain. She had the uncanny knack of attracting these seduction studs like bees to honey. Sweet words dripping into her ears undid her resistance to flattery faster than men could rip apart buttons or even Velcro. And too often—they did. Usually, her heart got shredded in the process.

Lexie imagined she was perhaps Marilyn Monroe, Norma Jean reincarnated. She didn't have to seduce. Men slithered to her side like hypnotized snakes. Only too late did she learn such men scented her love-hunger pheromones. They'd breathed words she hungered for, yet like ulcers in her heart, she bled for more tender words, words dripping with kindness, not just sex. They never seemed to be on the menu.

Humiliation turned to acid and ate through her stomach wall. The unholy hunger pains drove her straight to the microwave because the only thing left was frozen food. Running as fast as she could down the wrong road couldn't happen on an empty stomach—unthinkable.

Men's empty words ran circles in her brain like a gerbil on a wheel. Going full throttle and never getting anywhere, Lexie figured the only thing separating her from gerbil-dumb was the way she'd get off the wheel to go for food. Miserable in her stretched-to-the-limit skin, she decided food had become her toxic sedative. Bingeing didn't relieve her anxiety and longing.

From here on, she'd decide which words to swallow and which to toss in the trash. Sticky-fingered, exhausted, and humbled, Lexie dropped to her knees in front of the refrigerator, begging to be fed from a more-noble Source. She faced her love-word-food crisis squarely with the fridge door *shut*. She'd begged for an answer and waited to find out what it was.

Rumbling, crunching sounds tumbled in the icemaker. From the fridge door's cold-water spigot, a genie wriggled out, inhaled kitchen air, and swelled to his full height. His turban grazed the ceiling above the fridge.

"Your food prob getting the best of you?" queried the genie.

Shocked, Lexie scooted back, making room for the genie's strange pointy-toed shoes. Too stunned for even a single-word reply, she quaked and nodded.

"You know the drill," he thundered. "Three wishes. Make it snappy! I've got frozen-food complications you can't imagine."

Knowing this chance might never come again, Lexie summoned her courage: "1. LOVE, I've got a powerful hunger for love. 2. Discernment, I want the smarts to know the difference between a crock of cranberries and real-love words. 3. I want to wear the outfits in the skinny-clothes end of my closet."

The kitchen shook with the genie's hearty laugh. Unfolding his massive arms, he bent his turbaned head to eye her closely and clapped his hands in front of her face.

"Done!" The genie disappeared in a mysterious mist of dry ice.

The cloud dissipated into snowy flakes floating to the linoleum around her. Somehow constrained to the point of not being able to breathe, she struggled to stand and stumbled to the bathroom to look in the mirror. Lexie drew back in amazement.

From chin to hips, her body was encased in a heavy crock of defrosting cranberries. Crimson goo oozed around her face and shoulders. Her arms were trapped to her sides. Emblazoned across the crock were huge letters spelling REAL LOVE. Her legs squeezed into her skinniest pair of summer slacks made them pop at the seams. She studied her horrified self in the mirror.

The unfairness of being ripped off again—with words—choked her.

But wait, there was an upside to the tale!

It occurred to her that unless she learned to eat with her toes, there was no way she could feed herself. Habitual trips to the fridge or the microwave would be pointless. She'd get skinny enough to make the crock fall off. Meantime, she could lick cranberry goo to sustain herself.

Lexie remembered it takes 21 days to change a habit. It would only take that much time to shed the crock. The genie really had brought the answer she'd begged for to break her self-destructive-behavior patterns.

He did bring REAL LOVE!

It was tough…but it was real.

THE LAST ZEBRA

Amanda Luzzader

No, not stripes, old lioness, but black scars you carved in me.
Gangrene grooves of bitterness, born in your brutality.

Until that day in the schoolyard, I didn't know I was different.
Gray birds soared to a blue sky; I'm the only one who flinched.

Lazy, worthless, piece of shit. Words deep branded in me.
Roared so much, so loudly; only evil could echo thee.

"If you really loved me, you wouldn't be so bad."
Mother, I always loved you. You're the only one I had.

Love's not black and white for me, but always black and blue.
Doesn't matter the pain you had, you know you hurt me too.

Long before you joined the pride, you zebra suffered first.
Didn't slow you down much though from quenching inherent thirst.

Lioness, you bruised me. Taunted and betrayed me. Tore me at
    my heart.
But the greatest injury you ever gave? Instinct to hit, and hate,
    and harm.

In the trying moments, when I'm most in need of sleep,
I sense the lions' coming; up to me they hungry creep.

Bundle of soft warm flesh I hold—not a lion nor a zebra.
He is the infant man I love and he sweetly calls me mama.

Little darling helps me forget everything old lion thought.
Nature preying on my mind; I mustn't let myself be caught.

You made me your zebra, but I'll be damned before he's mine.
And if you never see us, take it as a sign.

Old lioness, I may be dumb,
but I am a zebra who will run,

and run,

and run.

PEARLS BEFORE SWINE

Eric Bishop

WHATEVER IT WAS, MY HORSE DIDN'T WANT ANY.

Krasher's ears were cocked forward at attention. Ten years of ranch life had taught him to relax—as much as a horse could. Most of the stuff he thought would kill him hadn't even made him tired, like the first time he carried a packsaddle. But horses were particular. Sometimes a thing they'd seen a hundred times scared the bejesus right out of 'em.

"That saddle's possessed," we'd joke as the horse went berserk. "Wasn't ever before, but it is right now."

The year I broke Krasher a stick carrying beaver in a swift river went right between his legs. He went bull-goose looney. Didn't stop bucking until I surfaced on the downstream side of the hole where he tossed me. He was on the bank, reins dangling to the ground, snorting at the beaver, who just kept swimming to wherever it had in mind for placing the stick. Then Krasher spooked almost as bad at my boots sloshing and the river dripping from my deformed Stetson.

There'd been plenty of trails since then, but right now he wouldn't go. I didn't think much of it. Perhaps the waning light scared him or the wind and the dark clouds overhead were chuck full of demons only he could see. I boot-heeled him, but all he'd do was back up, snort and strike with his front hooves.

A canopy of needles topped the arrow straight lodgepole pines surrounding us. Between the trunks were bushes and grass. A hundred feet ahead was a pile of boulders with a raspberry thicket halfway up. The thicket moved, and I realized what Krasher was so worked up over. Probably a black bear or some concealed critter. Krasher's instinct was to run, but I wanted some raspberries. A gunshot would scare a bear away easy enough, so I got off and tied Krasher to a tree.

"Nothin's gonna eat you."

He brushed me aside with the toss of his head as he kicked at the air with his hind legs. "Steady!" I scolded.

Krasher's ears and eyes focused on the boulders and then he went to yanking back so hard some pinecones fell, which scared him even worse. I feared he'd topple the tree, but it held and so did my tether.

"That'll be a dandy to untie," I grumbled in anticipation of how tight the knot would be.

A hissing squeal came from behind. I spun back toward the raspberries. Whatever it was hissed again. Krasher spun into me as I tried to unscabbard my rifle.

Wedged between two boulders beside the thicket was fur. All matted with mud, some animal must've crawled into the crack to die. But if it truly was dead, what had just made the hissing sound? I hadn't noticed the fur from the horse, but the change in angle from saddleback to feet could account for that. Not wanting Krasher to live up to his name again, I decided against the Winchester and palmed the six-shooter from my hip.

A grouse exploded beneath my feet halfway to the boulders. His wings beat the air until he landed on a tree branch. I was half tempted to shoot him from the perch, but I wanted raspberries not grouse for dinner.

When I looked again at the boulders, the fur was gone.

Whatever it was should have left tracks, but when I got to the boulders there wasn't a single one. The bushes were plucked free of berries. Smeared mud, warm to my touch and still damp, marked the boulders where I'd spotted the fur.

Some twigs snapped somewhere to my left.

A lightning strike lit up the sky, and the attendant thunder boomed in the same instant.

Something big was running away from me through the woods.

"Git back here!" I yelled as Krasher galloped, clipping trees and breaking branches in his wake. I spun, scanning all about until my eyes rested on the tree where I'd tied the horse. It only took seconds to run to the spot, where I found horseshoe tracks surrounding the tree, but no lead rope.

Something with a fencing-plier strong thumb had untied the knot; that same thumb might now be wrapped around my Winchester.

I dropped to the ground.

Rain started, but I lay still as thimble-sized drops smacked my shirt. It built to a downpour, eventually soaking through my Stetson and running down my neck. I stayed. If the trigger of my own gun was going to be pulled on me, I wasn't going to give the shooter a daytime target. That was the plan, and I stuck to it even though the wind started and the soaked clothing against my skin went from cool to freezing. Then it went to hailing. The pebble-sized ice balls stung my back. Shaking started in my teeth, and I clinched my jaw against the chattering.

My stomach growled. The jerky and biscuits in my saddlebags would've been good. Hopefully Krasher had found his way to a meadow with tall grass.

Night brought more rain and lightning. The woods went from pitch-black to bright as noon with each strike. The forest would light up, and I'd try to look at a different spot to study how best to make my run. There was never enough time for my mind to soak in the entire picture. Was that a tree, a rock, or something else? Noises came from all about. Thunder would crack and the world got bright, but everything looked different than it had in the daylight. During one of the longest strikes, a bearded man dressed in pelts stood twenty feet away. I pointed my six-shooter, but when the woods lit up the next instant, what I thought was the man was a tree trunk covered with fuzzy moss. The lightning stopped and everything went gravedigger dark and then quiet until the wind picked up again. Trees rubbing against each other, sticks cracking, and the wind whistling through the forest piled ugly pictures into my head.

The moon came out from behind a sucker hole in the clouds, casting enough light to see. I picked out a hundred-year-old pine fifty feet ahead that had to be at least four-feet thick. If no bullets came, and I made it, I'd keep going for the boulders where I'd seen the shaking bushes.

The hiss came from the place where I swore I'd seen the caveman.

I jumped from the ground, six-shooter in hand and ran for all I had. Nearing the tree, something ran like my shadow in the periphery to the right. I wondered if what I saw was my shadow, but it couldn't be because the moon was shining the opposite direction. Every hair on my body stood straight up. I glanced and it sped toward me. I veered, hoping to angle away but it closed the gap like a mountain lion after a calf. When my lungs and legs gave out, I cocked the hammer, spun and stopped in one motion.

My breathing gusted in and out. If I could only slow it down and get quiet perhaps I could blend into the shadows. Whatever it was must have stopped with me. Clouds moved over the moon and I couldn't see anything. My lungs burned, but I held my breath listening.

Nothing.

I fired at movement to my left. The gunshot exposed my position. A branch snapped behind so I spun and shot rounds two and three. A rock hit my mouth. I stayed on my feet with blood spilling from my split lips onto my chin. The next rock glanced off my shoulder and I spun to shoot the fourth, fifth, and sixth rounds into nothing. I worked a bullet from my belt loop and thumbed open the revolver's trap door. I dropped the bullet in the cylinder. Something sprang from the ground at my side. It walloped me like a mule kick. I fumbled the gun. It was at my neck. We thrashed tooth and fingernail. Me against something fur covered and a foot taller than my six feet. I tried for my knife but a hand closed around my forearm before I could take it from the scabbard. The bones snapped and my hand went numb. It threw me to the ground like I was no heavier than a scarecrow. My good hand palmed a rock, perhaps the one that had been thrown at me. It was torn from my grasp. A blow to the chest busted my ribs and knocked me to my belly. It was on top of me. Two more blows across the back of my head left me woozy. My lungs screamed for air that wouldn't enter, and I thrashed like a fish out of water until the lighter places blended into the darker ones.

I woke, surprised to be alive. Blood was still running from my mouth and head. What breathing I could muster crackled and popped in my chest. I tried to sit but was too weak, so I looked at the stars and palmed the dirt and pine needles with my un-crippled hand. My knife and gun were gone. I spent the next hour too battered to move more than a few inches, while worrying over my broken arm and the lifeless hand. Coughing became a spasm and stabbing pain in my ribcage. It brought blood to my mouth that I swallowed, too short of breath to spit past my chin. Sleep eventually vanquished the pain.

Warm breath in my face woke me at dawn. I panicked, kicking and squirming, igniting fire in my forearm and chest as the bone ends jabbed inside. The attacker had returned. I was sure. But then I recognized the snort and Krasher's silhouette. The saddle was beneath his belly and the Winchester was gone, but my bedroll was still fastened behind the cantle.

Using the horn and rigging for handles, I pulled myself up and righted the saddle with my good arm and took off the blankets and canvas. I wrapped up as tight as I could in the blankets and shivered myself warm. Sticks cracked, but Krasher stood statue still, unworried by the forest's noises as the sun rose. Between bouts of coughing, I splinted my arm with two branches, using my neckerchief for a wrapping.

Krasher stood, steady as the rising sun, for me to climb aboard.

Krasher stepped out strong and purposeful, with me so weak, I couldn't have fought through wet paper. My swollen lips, scrapes under my torn shirt and several lumps on my head only started the list. It was all becoming distant as Krasher moved, jostling aches that came to me like telegraphs from a distant place. We crossed a stream and rounded a bend into a meadow.

The morning rays cast long shadows, warming the night's dew into rising steam and traces of rainbows.

I hacked up a mouthful of blood that splattered over Krasher's mane and neck. More coughing stifled my breathing and then everything went numb. When I woke, Krasher stood over me. Something rustled to the left, as I hacked more blood. The hiss came from the tall grass, but I couldn't even roll. Then everything went warm, even my lifeless hand, as Krasher snorted and spun smacking the earth with his front hooves.

I blinked against the collapsing world. The tall grass shook and Krasher bolted away. I watched him disappear through reverse telescope vision into a tiny spot of bright light.

Atta boy. I thought. *Save yourself. I should've listened. Maybe the next cowboy will.* I no longer felt, smelled, heard or saw anything except death's final notice. *Swine and pearls come in all shapes and sizes.*

AS A MAN THINKETH...SO IS HE

Margie Broschinsky

I have thought to ponder carefully the ideas man conceives
Except he is attentive, he may be easily deceived
The reality of my unfolding, for each of us is true
The thoughts I choose direct my life and yours do the same for you

A senseless man may speculate that his thoughts are not affecting
But, without careful concentration, he may find himself reflecting
On a choice—which once fulfilled—and has left him broken-hearted—
Reveals this painful truth: The thought is where the conduct started

It is foolish to be idle and allow our minds to wander
This choice invites our enemy to direct the things we ponder
His tactics are deceptive and commence if we permit
Then we, not he, will bear the blame for acts that we commit

Once ensnared by evil's deceit, it is difficult to escape
Of our free will, we made the choice and our minds can recreate
Reminding us of our adventures and the novel fascination
And encouraging just one more journey to the destructive destination

But, in time, there is no doubt, man will tragically recall
The first step that was taken toward the devastating fall
Sadly he will remember walking willingly to this spot
And recognize that the choice was preceded by a thought

SWIMMING WITH THE SHARKS

Marilyn Richardson

CANCER FREE ARE WORDS EVERYONE DIAGNOSED WITH CANCER waits to hear. Not, "Your cancer is in remission," but "Cancer free"—although the former is more likely the truer statement.

In either case, I'm not there yet. I've completed the fourth of the four chemo treatments recommended by my doctor, but haven't yet started the 5 ½ weeks of radiation to be followed by the five years of estrogen blocker pills.

To be honest, I'm not sure the cure isn't worse than the disease.

I'm grateful to all those who call, send cards, express their love and concern. People are really terrific. Still I continue to be amazed that people who know nothing about the effects of the chemo tell me that I am strong, that I can do it, that I should finish the treatment. They tell me to be brave, implying that it is worth whatever I must endure. I know they think that if I don't follow through, my chances for beating the cancer are lessened, but it seems such a crapshoot anyway. No one can tell you if this will work. And they definitely don't know what my response to the chemo has been.

THROWN TO THE SHARKS

The first two infusions had seemed like a lark although they had their ups and downs. I spent three days in the hospital after the first one because my white count went to zip. But after the first day, when I was pretty weak, I loved being in the hospital. The food was great, the service A1 and I felt cared for.

Following the third infusion on a Thursday, something else happened. I'd fallen into bed around 7:30 on Friday night, and slept for ten hours, woke up for half an hour, hungry and thirsty and in need of a bath. Without moving I fell back to sleep for several more hours, waking now and then to consider how thirsty and hungry I was. I lay there, helpless, weak, immobile.

Even though there was a glass of water next to me with a straw, the act of reaching for the glass, lifting it to my lips and taking a sip was beyond me. I tried to tell my husband that I needed help, but his nature is such that he'd as likely spit in your face as intrude into your personal space without a verbal invitation. So I imagined a scenario to describe my situation.

I've been thrown from a ship into a shark filled sea. The night is pitch-black. As I sail through the air toward the water I hear a voice call out, "Swim north." Since I have no idea which way is north, I just keep paddling, turning on my back now and then, to rest. I don't feel pain. I just swim little stokes and waited for the sharks.

I recite the above scene over and over in my head, wishing it were more clever, more descriptive. That maybe, by repeating it enough times, something more creative will come to mind, but nothing does.

Questioning why I was so unprepared for this reaction to the chemo, I decide there must be a strong belief in the theory that if you tell a patient how bad it might be, they'll live out that worst of scenarios. But to suggest I be good to myself, that the fatigue is cumulative, to rest as I needed, was absolutely worthless advice.

LIVING FOREVER

The Huntsman Cancer center is well funded and well staffed. When first diagnosed you are flooded with mini workshops, meetings, classes on make-up (when you look better you feel better), free wigs and hats, handouts, booklets, cards with numbers to call, an exercise class to prevent lymphedema, a swelling in the arm that if it comes never goes away. But once the chemo starts, you are on your own. I guess the support staff assumes if you need something you'll call. But if you can't pick up glass of water, you can't pick up the phone.

Someone should invent a new word for *chemo fatigue.* When you are tired, you rest and you feel better. No amount of sleep cures this fatigue—and when I finally had enough energy to sit and up and Google the term, I read that the fatigue may last for several months following the end of chemo. For some people it lasts a year and for others it never goes away.

With the best of intentions friends and relatives tell you about all the people they know who have been declared cancer free. They tell about marvelous clinics in Southern California and Arizona where you can go for natural cures. But soon, and without realizing it, they drift into telling about someone they know whose cancer returned, who…then they catch themselves, apologize and change the subject.

In the television series *Sex and the City*, the character Samantha suffers hot flashes, becomes a spokesperson, takes off her wig in public, but never is there a word about the effects of the chemo.

I've made a list of my side effects. It is surprising how many there are yet how short their duration: pink flush, painfully dry left nostril, nasty tasting water, tingling feet, hair loss, shooting pains, pains in hip and knee joints, interrupted sleep, watering eyes, red splotches on my skin, discoloration and sensitivity of fingernails (will they fall off?), feet painful to walk on, shedding of skin, especially the feet, and the need to sleep and sleep and sleep yet wake up still exhausted.

With my type A personality, everyone thought I'd do well. My good doctor explained that my intense reaction was unusual. But no one can tell me if the chemo and radiation will actually kill all the cancer cells. When I ask about that my doctor says that the only way to know is if the cancer comes back.

I wasn't sure I could withstand the fourth (and final) infusion. The doctor agreed to reduce the chemicals by 30 percent. If she'd said only 20 percent I was prepared to say no thanks. I did fine.

I keep thinking that I don't have to live forever. After all, I'm 78. I read the obits and see that people die at 73, 76, 62. Lots of people are pleased to announce that they have beaten cancer, but Robin Roberts, of ABC's *Good Morning America* had her cancer return as leukemia. Steve Jobs lost his battle.

I heard on the news recently that the survival rate of five years following breast cancer diagnosis had increased from 50 percent in the 70s, to 85 percent now. So I'll focus on living a full life for as long as it lasts, but I know for sure that I'm not going to do chemo again, no matter what.

SQUIRRELS

Lorraine Jeffery

I imagine I can feel it—
the wood stock against my shoulder,
the cold steel of the trigger and,
      I'm squeezing, squeezing…

Actually, I'm a peaceful person.
      I've never shot an animal
      for food or sport.
But this is war and I'm losing
      the defensive line
      of my backyard.

The enemy sits with claws
embedded in tree bark,
battle tails raised,
watching with
black beady eyes.

They are waiting
until I let down my guard,
and then they will eat my tomatoes, pears,
tulip bulbs, apples, daffodils, seed corn
strawberries, birdseed and anything else
in their march through the yard.
      Hell, pigs are pickier!

Digging foxholes,
the enemy's divisions move rapidly.
They are the backhoes of the
animal world.

I've tried treaties with mothballs,
    deception with traps,
    and now I'm moving to
    the heavy artillery.

It would be easy.
Pow! They're gone.
Maybe I'd feel guilty later—
    but I doubt it.

GRANDFATHER

Emily Younker

JAMES HOVERED AT THE ENTRANCE TO THE NURSING HOME AND rocked back and forth on his heels. He gripped the straps of his backpack and scurried farther into the room. The woman at the desk looked up.

"Can I help you?"

"I'm here to visit my grandfather." He let go of the straps and stuffed his hands in his pocket.

"Is he expecting you?"

James nodded. "I know where his room is. Can I go see him?"

"Of course. Don't forget, visiting hours end at five."

James hurried down the hall and looked into the rooms. In one room an older man sat alone. He stared out the window watching the snow drift down on the already white landscape. The man's cotton white hair was combed back. The man turned to look at James.

"Do I know you?"

James gave a nervous laugh. "Grandpa, don't you remember? It's Parents' Night at the Junior High. I'm here to pick you up."

The grandfather rubbed his jaw. "Tonight?"

James clenched his hands then forced them open. "Yes. Our ride is coming in five minutes. We'll be back by eight."

The old man stared at him.

James's smile faded for a moment. "Grandpa?"

"Help me with my coat, Harold."

"James. My name is James"

"Your parents gave you the wrong name. Go get my coat, Harold. It is in the closet."

When the grandfather had his coat on, James lent his arm and they walked out the side door. The snow still drifted down and they shuffled along the sidewalk. The grandfather looked up and let out a chuckle.

"Makes me dizzy looking at all of the snow falling down. I remember when I lived on the farm, we use to make paths through the snow to get to the barns."

James's heart slowed as he listened to the stories. A car pulled up and James hurried the grandfather into his classmate's car. At the school, James and the grandfather shuffled down the hall to the home room class. James hovered in the door, flushing, and stuffed his hands in his pockets. He felt a hand on his shoulder and looked up.

"Harold, keep your head up. Remember, I am here."

They sat down and James found himself sitting across from Nick and his suit-dressed father.

"Who's this?" Nick asked.

"I'm Harold's grandfather."

"You mean James."

"You may call him James. But to me he will always be Harold."

"Weirdo. He doesn't have a grandfather," Nick said.

"Think about that statement for a moment and then tell it to me again."

James looked at the old man who winked. The teacher came in and the evening commenced. James read his latest story and showed his art projects to the grandfather. As they talked, James forgot for a moment the fact that he wasn't like the other students.

"Excuse me, but there has been a problem."

James's head snapped up as the officer walked into the room. He glanced at the old man and felt all his fears come crashing down.

"What's wrong?" his teacher asked.

"There has been a kidnapping. We need to return Mr. Johnson to the nursing home." The orderly moved past the officer and headed towards their table. "Come with me, Mr. Johnson."

Nick turned to look at James. "Kidnapping? Seriously?"

James's face burned and he stared at the table. His mother was working, as usual. He walked by the nursing home every day on his way home from school. It had been easy to ask his coworker for a ride. All he had to do was find a willing accomplice to pretend to be family for the evening.

Mr. Johnson, that was his name, spoke. "I am sorry, but I'm spending the evening with my grandson. I'll be back by eight."

"Mr. Johnson, you don't have any family. You're a bachelor."

"You're wrong. I do have a family. This is my grandson, Harold. If you would excuse me, we have some catching up to do. I was told I could go out for family visits whenever I wanted to so long as I was back on time. It is only seven."

The orderly and officer talked for a moment and then took a seat at the back of the room.

When the evening ended the cop gave James and Mr. Johnson a ride back to the nursing home. The nurse followed. James helped Mr. Johnson back to his room. The officer followed them in.

"I'm sorry about kidnapping you. But thank you," James said.

"Anytime you need a grandfather, let me know."

"Would you mind if I came by tomorrow? I mean, if you don't have anything else to do?"

"I would love that. Have a nice evening, James."

BLUE BALLOON

Robyn Buttars

Blue Balloon bounced away
With the wind. Off to play.

Darted straight. Crossed the lawn.
Skipped the fence. It was gone.

Flashed the sky like a spark.
Lunged to land in the park.

Pirouette through the trees.
Two-step trot on the breeze.

Hooked the swing for a ride,
Back and forth—easy glide.

Jigged upon jungle gym.
Teeteered wild on the brim.

Pummeled down, bopped the ground.
Spinner swirled round and round.

Hopped atop monkey bars.
Dove to drive kiddy cars.

Climbed the steps. Shot the slide.
Burrowed deep—tunnel hide.

Whipped again end on end.
Through the park, round the bend.

Vaulted one windy blast—
Cleared the fence. Home at last.

BOMBS AND BLIND DATES

Chris Todd Miller

A PILE OF SHREDDED NAPKINS SAT IN FRONT OF AMANDA. She reached for another, intent on increasing the pile, then pushed it all away. That's just what she needed—to have him show up and find her nurturing a small pulp farm. She concealed the torn remnants with her menu, which was a formality anyway. She'd told herself she'd only get a salad but knew that somehow their five-star mushroom burger would find her plate.

She glanced out the window, past her police cruiser (she'd taken a small liberty and parked in a loading zone), and toward the county courthouse. Friday evening at a government job meant most people had left hours ago, but a few occupants still trickled out as Lady Justice punched the clock. Amanda felt an odd sort of symmetry: her ex-husband, Hal, had an office across the street. In a few minutes she would meet a blind date in the same café where she and Hal had first met.

Tonight was her first date in more than a year and her first blind date in nearly five. Well, it was supposed to be a blind date, but she'd run a background check. Even off the clock, a cop is always a cop. As such, she found the butterflies in her stomach a bit of a surprise. She had no expectations. Next semester, she'd start night courses on her way to a law degree and her dating life would go from critical care to code blue.

"Another Diet Coke, ma'am?" her server asked.

"Sure. Thanks." She pushed her glass to him. "With lemon, and could you…" she lifted the menu. "Sorry."

"No problem." He scooped up the napkin remains and left with her glass.

"Amanda?"

She looked over her shoulder at six feet of a not-too-shabby-for-a-blind-date date. Better than his picture. She smiled. "Yes. And you must be Gregory."

"Guilty," he said.

Strike one.

He sat down across from her. "Call me Greg. Do you go by Mandy?"

"Not if you want to get lucky. Ever."

Greg raised his eyebrows and leaned back with his hands in the surrender position.

"Sorry," she said. "I can be a little brash when I'm nervous."

Greg leaned forward and interlaced his fingers. "That's all right. I appreciate a candid response, especially on a first date."

"Not that I mean you're getting lucky tonight, or any night. I mean, well, maybe." She sighed. "Just call me Amanda."

"Noted. It looks like we'll be able to dispense with the standard first date thrust-and-parry and get right to the actual people behind our best-behavior personas."

She noticed his emphasis of the word thrust, but gave him a pass. She did mention sex first, after all. "You're breaking all sorts of first date etiquette."

"Just you wait," he said with a smirk and a raise of his eyebrow.

Their server returned with her drink. "Can I get you a beverage, sir?"

"I'll have a Hefeweizen." He looked to Amanda. "Anything for you, besides the Diet Coke, I take it?"

"No thanks. I don't drink on the first date."

He gave her a look that she couldn't quite decipher. The server began to leave when Greg stopped him. "We're ready to order."

"We are?" Amanda asked.

"Trust me. I'm good at this," Greg said.

She shook her head. "What would Ms. Manners say?"

Letting any man order for her was a stretch, but there was something about him that appealed to her.

Strike two, but call it a foul tip.

"We'll have egg croustades, spinach soufflé, and stuffed crepes."

The server listened and nodded, then left to get the beer.

Amanda raised an eyebrow. "Croustades? Soufflé? Stuffed crepes? For dinner? You might get lucky, after all," she chuckled.

The explosion from across the street rattled the windows of the café. Amanda felt the expelled energy and for a moment, she couldn't breathe.

People along the street and on the courthouse grounds screamed, running in every direction. Panic colored their faces. Cars screeched and collided as drivers tried to avoid desperate pedestrians. A dust cloud emerged from a gaping hole in the middle of the courthouse. She couldn't be sure but it looked as though the fourth floor had collapsed along with most of the third.

"Dear God in heaven," Amanda muttered.

Images from the Boston marathon and 9/11 flashed in her mind. She jumped up from the table and took a swig of Greg's beer. "I'll take a rain check."

"I'll call you."

She pushed past the gawkers in the doorway and went straight to her car. From the trunk she grabbed a police radio and her custom emergency kit. She slung it over her shoulder. Precious seconds ticked by. She clipped the body of the walkie-talkie to her belt and the receiver to the strap of the first aid kit near her neck, then added her badge and side arm, a .40 caliber Beretta. Who knew what she'd find once she got across the street?

Scores of people ran from the chaos; Amanda fought her way to the middle of it.

At the front steps, she paused to make a quick assessment. The main floor and the second still stood, but there was no way to know if the blast had weakened them.

A man covered in dust and wearing what was probably a thousand dollar suit, staggered toward her. Blood ran down the side of his face. She grabbed a gauze bandage from her bag and pressed it to his head.

"Sir, what's your name?"

His head bobbled. She grabbed his hand and placed it on the bandage, then repeated her inquiry.

"Stan," he said. "My name's Stan."

She led him down the steps. "Stan, I need you to hold this bandage to your head. Can you do that?"

The cool air seemed to give him his bearings. "Yeah," he said. "I think I'm okay now."

Dark storm clouds roiled and blew Amanda's hair into her face, odd how she hadn't noticed the storm until now. She paused to tie back her hair then turned and dashed into the building. Dust mixed with the air creating a haze. She coughed but kept moving. Thanks to her numerous court appearances, she knew the layout. The folks, who hadn't clocked out early, ambled about like extras on the *Walking Dead*. She directed them to the nearest exit. A couple of times she stopped to administer first aid, but for everyone on the ground floor, their wounds looked superficial. She kept pressing forward to the center of the blast where she suspected she'd find people in greater need of assistance.

The emergency stairwell in the back remained intact, although she could see hairline cracks in the concrete steps and the walls. She tempered her urgency and took great care in her ascent. The stairs proved reliable enough to get her to the third floor—Hal's floor.

The arm bar of the third floor door clicked open when she leaned against it but the door stopped after a couple of inches. Emergency lighting from the stairwell didn't illuminate much of the hallway. Amanda inhaled and she froze. Natural gas—faint, but unmistakable. Her heart beat double-time as her fight or flight response kicked in.

Flight. Definitely.

She took two steps, heard something, and stopped. She tilted her head, listening.

"Somebody, help me. Is anybody there?"

Like the gas, the outcry was weak, but unmistakable.

Wary that any electrical charge, even a cell phone, could set off the gas, she keyed her mic. "Central, this is Officer Adcock, badge number 4785. I'm in the Merridian County courthouse. Be advised of a gas leak in the building. I suspect you're already aware of the explosion."

"Emergency and rescue units are en route. You are instructed to evacuate."

"Negative, Central. I hear someone calling for help. I'm going farther in."

A new voice came over the radio. "Adcock, get your ass out of there immediately."

"Is that you, Captain?"

"Damn straight. I'm outside with a team of structural engineers, but we can't do shit until the gas is contained and neither can you."

"Get Public Works to turn off the gas. Shut down the whole block if you have to," Amanda said. "Engineers are fine, but my gut says we'll need an excavation crew."

"They're working on the gas," Captain Cayhill replied.

"Tell them to work faster. If you want me, you'll have to come and get me. Adcock out."

Not wanting to risk a flashlight, she pulled a light stick from the emergency kit, cracked it and shook until a soft green glow emerged. She looked into the hallway. Broken glass and concrete lay strewn about. Amanda put her shoulder against the door, grunted and pushed. She heard scraping and the door gave six inches.

She squeezed herself through. "Hello?" Dust casually swirled about her.

"Help. Down here."

She rounded a corner and continued down a hallway toward the epicenter of the blast—a jagged hole in the center of the building half a football field wide. The voice came from that end. An ache grew in her stomach as she maneuvered under dangling fluorescent lights and around pieces of desks, tables, and crumbling walls. She knew this hallway. About thirty feet from the drop off, she stopped at an office door that read: Hal A. Adcock, ADA.

Civic duty notwithstanding, she'd known since entering the building that this was her destination. They didn't hate each other. They still kind of liked each other. Even at the lowest point of their marriage, she'd never wished anything like this on him. "Hal?"

No reply.

Time seemed to stand still. She stood in the doorway of the waiting room and took in the scene. Half of the room was gone, literally gone. She looked past the remnants to the void and the open offices, like looking at a dollhouse with the rooms cut away. Office furniture—desks, copiers, computers, and chairs—had either tumbled into the pit or dangled from their cords, any of which could yank free and release a spark.

A black sky encroached on the blown-out roof. The winds blew legal briefs and assorted paperwork about the cavity that used to be the courthouse. The fresh air gave her goose bumps. It also diluted the gas so she and Hal wouldn't pass out—but they could still blow up.

"Hal, where are you?"

"Mandy? Oh, thank God. Back here."

She picked her way past the reception area to his office, which was also missing a wall. Hal lay pinned under an oak desk that wasn't his. Chairs sat with their legs in the air. Shards of glass from wall frames cut through crinkled diplomas and certificates. The golf clubs she'd given him for their last anniversary stood in the corner, somehow unscathed. She shook her head and knelt next to him. "Where are you hurt?"

He half smiled, half grimaced at her.

"What?" she asked.

"I always knew you'd come back."

"You could've just called."

"What? No kiss?" he asked.

Bits of ceiling tile speckled his hair. She brushed them away then shined a penlight into each of his eyes, checking for a concussion. "I'd tell you to kiss my ass, but then you'd just fall in love with me again and I don't need that."

"It'd be worth it. I'd die a happy man."

"You're not gonna die. I won't let you lay that on me," she said.

"Here's what I do know. One leg is broken and maybe the hip, but I'm not entirely sure since I can't feel my legs at the moment."

Amanda sighed. "Okay, now for more good news. The hallway's like a boot camp obstacle course and the back stairs are iffy at best. We should be able to get you out from under there," she nodded at the desk, "and I can fireman-carry you out of here."

"Always the optimist," he said.

"You haven't changed either. Still lying there, expecting me to do all the work."

He laughed until he coughed up blood. A couple of drops stained his shirt.

It was good to hear him laugh, but not like this. "Oh, and there's a gas leak," she said.

"Gas, huh?" He paused.

For a moment she thought he'd passed out, then he spoke.

"Don't get me wrong, this is super romantic with the mood lighting and all, but let's call this what it is."

"The punch line to a lawyer joke?" she asked.

"Bottom of the ninth. Two out. Nobody on."

"I thought you hated baseball, especially analogized," she said.

"True, but you love baseball. You should go. Get out while you can."

She leaned back, touched by his selfless gesture, but she couldn't let him know that. "Shut your face. I abandoned stuffed crepes to be here."

He rolled his eyes.

"Hey." Her sharp tone made him look at her again and she adopted a serious tone. "Don't worry. Mariano's on the mound.

He always gets the save."

She moved to the other side of the office where she could hear better and spoke into her radio. "Cayhill, you there?"

"Adcock, where are you?" His voice sounded tinny and distant.

"Third floor. My ex-husband's office. He's in bad shape." She looked over at him. He lay with his eyes closed; even in the low light his face looked pale.

"How'd you get to the third floor?"

"I went up the back staircase."

"The gas is off, but until it dissipates, the building's not considered clear. And one other thing."

"What?"

"The engineers did an exterior inspection."

"And?"

"That stairwell you used? From the outside it looks compromised. I can't advise you to use it again. I can order you to evacuate, immediately."

She wanted to ask him how he proposed she do that. "The stairwell's not my preferred exit, anyway. Hal's pinned down. He's got some serious injuries." She relayed his condition.

"What do you have in mind?" Cayhill asked.

"Air evac."

"Are you insane? Even if there was no gas, a chopper would hardly stand a chance against these winds."

"I know." She kept her voice even.

"You want someone to maintain a chopper in the wind alongside a crumbling building while you strap your ex to a stretcher?"

"That's the long and short of it."

"You are insane."

"Agreed. Do you see any other options?"

He sighed. "Let me make some calls."

"Thanks, and uh, you know, don't take all night."

"Yeah, that's what she said. Cayhill out."

Amanda stepped back to Hal and gave him a bottle of water

from her emergency kit. "We need to get you free."

He waved her off. "Mandy, we both know how this ends. Go."

Ah, yes, this is why we divorced. But this time, you're not in charge. "Well, Henry, you don't get to make that decision. It's a moot point anyway. The staircase is no longer an option, and they won't approve a chopper for just little ol' me."

"A chopper?"

"We're going out the roof." *I hope. Come on, Cayhill.* She positioned herself next to the desk. "I'll lift, you drag. Can you handle that?"

"Sure and while I'm at it I'll draft up a proposal for world peace."

She gave him a look, one she'd used often during their marriage. "You can be a real pussy sometimes, you know that?" She squatted next to the desk and positioned her fingers under the edge. He propped his hands against the floor. "Count of three: one, two, three." Straining the muscles in her arms and back, she groaned but managed to lift the oak desk about a foot. Hal pushed against the floor and cried out in pain, gaining about six inches, until his palms slipped and he dropped onto his elbows.

"Come on, baby," Amanda said. "Just a little bit farther."

He scrunched up his face, took a deep breath and pulled himself free.

Amanda dropped the desk. It hit the floor with a thud and she rolled back to a sitting position just as an office chair toppled over the jagged edge of the floor.

"Does crying like a little girl get my man card revoked?" Hal asked.

Amanda's radio hissed. "Adcock are you there?"

She took a moment to catch her breath before keying the mic. "And where would I have gone?"

Sulfur still lingered on the air and its odor bit into her tongue.

"Chopper's on its way. ETA, ten minutes," Cayhill replied.

She looked into the crevasse left by the blast and eyed all of the destroyed equipment and exposed wires. "Two would be better," she said under her breath.

"Stuffed crepes, huh?" Hal asked. "For dinner? You were on a date."

"Jealous?"

"I think we're past that now, don't you?" he asked.

"I do." She nodded. "We're past a lot of things."

"That may only be the second time I've heard the words *I do* from your mouth. Both times you were saving my life," he said.

"This is no time to go nostalgic." *Please, no. Now was no time to go digging up the past.*

A new voice came over the radio. She said a silent thank you for the interruption.

"Officer Adcock, this is Lieutenant Sparks of the Merridian County Search and Helicopter Rescue."

Sparks? The irony of his name made Amanda wince.

"I have the courthouse in my sights. What's your position?"

"Third floor, northeast corner. Look for the green glow."

"Copy that."

She turned to Hal. "Help's on the way. Hang in there." She pulled out the remaining glow sticks and placed them about the blown out office.

"We have to immobilize your legs for the stretcher."

Hal nodded.

She looked about the room and spied his golf bag. Grabbing a couple of irons and a roll of athletic tape from her bag, she went about splinting his legs.

Across the void, an orange fireball exploded in the remnants of an office.

"Shit." Amanda scrambled backward and covered her eyes, expecting a larger explosion. Ten seconds passed. She didn't die. Exposure to the wind and proximity from the main leak kept the explosion small and contained.

She keyed her mic. "Sparks, quit doing your nails get us the fuck out of here."

"Approaching the building now," he replied.

Hal chuckled. "You always cuss when you're stressed. I like that about you."

She glared at him then looked up to see the chopper lowering into the void. An orange stretcher dangled from a rope and spun in the wind. She spoke into the radio. "Bring it closer."

"The gusts are something fierce up here," Sparks said. "Hang on."

The urgency in his voice cut through the airwaves. Amanda watched as the stretcher bobbed and spun until it neared their position. She lunged at it and missed. Momentum nearly cast her over the edge. Her heart and uvula met in the back of her throat as she windmilled her arms desperately trying to regain her balance. She found it and stepped a few paces back. Sparks made another pass with the stretcher, but she was out of reach and it spun away.

"Damn it. Okay, what else? What else?" Her eyes darted around the room then fell on Hal. Keying her mic, she said, "Sparks, give me two minutes."

Her radio crackled. "Make it one."

Standing over Hal, she took off his belt.

"What are you doing?"

Then, removed her own. "Easy, cowboy." She stepped away and grabbed the putter from his bag. Latching the end of one belt to the buckle of the other, she then looped the entire thing around the leg of the oak desk. Grasping the free end with one hand and the putter in her other, she leaned back testing the weight of the desk. Convinced it would hold, she radioed Sparks then leaned out over the expanse. The void looked as though it was waiting for her to fall into its maw and be devoured. Her heart raced. Extending the putter, she snagged the rope on the first try. Pulling against the belts, she brought herself back into the office and secured the stretcher.

Sparks came over the radio. "Strap him in and then climb into the harness."

"Copy that," Amanda replied.

"I can't believe you did that," Hal said.

She moved the stretcher next to him. "You should see what I do with leftovers."

Hal positioned himself over the side of the stretcher in a sitting position. He was sweating and breathing rapidly—signs of shock, probably from internal bleeding. They were running out of time. "Just swing my legs in," he said.

She heard panic in his voice, saw it in his eyes. They both knew they should probably already be dead. She grabbed his ankles. "Ready?"

"Ready."

With two steps, she swung his legs in place and pulled the straps tight. He grimaced, clenching his jaw. For now, she was glad he couldn't feel his legs. She stepped into the harness and snapped it over her shoulders and thighs then clipped into the carabineer above the stretcher.

"Sparks, two for evac. Go!"

"Copy that."

The stretcher jerked into the crevasse. The winds pushed the helicopter about like it was a plaything sent in just for them. She could only imagine what Sparks was doing to keep them from colliding with the building.

As they rose out of the debris Hal yelled, "I'm still in love with you."

Amanda smiled and grabbed his hand. "Don't make me drop you."

He shook his head. "I won't."

A LUFTWAFFE PILOT REMEMBERS

Lorraine Jeffery

Belief
    the shimmer of steel as
    wings tipped, and stukas
    screamed towards the ground.
    Jericho's trumpets indeed.

Love
    thrumming heartbeat of the engines
    with brothers in the air.
    Black forests and flowing
    ribbon of the Elbe.
    Swastikas and Beethoven

Pride
    Strong Aryan soldiers flash in sunlight
    Goering's mind—bright with strategies
    Visions from the Reich
    Young fliers owning the skies
    Horizon of shining futures

I flew like the eagle
    on my breast, over Poland, France,
    Belgium, Scandinavia—all of Europe.
    Only stogy Britain remained.

Doubt
> Black Thursday
> Rumors of Jewish camps
> Operation Barbarossa
> Fuel shortage
> Berlin in ruins

Grief
> Oh Dresden
> Death camps
> Hatred
> Shame
> Everything is gone,
>> but remembered.

THE PALLBEARERS

Chadd VanZanten

WE ALL COME TOGETHER AT THE CHURCH AROUND NINE IN THE morning. And I mean all of us. All six brothers, Sis, all the grand-kids. Val's kids are down from Vancouver. Dutch's son is in the States on furlough. We all descend on this little empty church on the edge of some tiny town where no one knows us.

The viewing doesn't start for six hours and there's fifteen cars in the parking lot already.

I pull the front door open and my kids duck under my arm and go inside. Jenny rushes in behind them, holding her hair in place because the wind is blowing like mad.

Before I go in I make sure I've got Dad's letter in my suit coat pocket.

Everyone looks old to me. Val's over sixty—he's got kids older than me. His hair is completely white now, and he walks slower than I remember.

Dutch stands in the foyer with his arms folded across his big chest. Probably the first one there. He's taken charge, like he always does when Dad's not around. I wonder if he knows about the letter.

"Chapel's right through there," says Dutch.

No, he doesn't know.

"Yeah, Dutch, I've been in a church before," I say.

"Wiseass." His neck is too thick for the top button of his shirt, so he tightens his tie periodically to conceal the gap.

Jenny kisses my cheek and goes in with the kids. Val and his people stream in behind us. They're all very tall. Val has eight kids, all grown, and some of them have kids. They have to stoop to hug us hello, as if they're of some alien race.

"Chapel's right through there," Dutch tells them, "and the bathrooms are down this hall on your right."

After they've gone I ask Dutch, "You know why Dad wanted to be buried out here instead of Boise?"

"I assumed he wanted to be a pain in the ass. What do you know about it?"

I shrug. It's not convincing.

He says, "Why didn't you shave this morning? It's a funeral. I mean criminy."

Sis leads Mom in, steadying her by the elbow. Mom blinks at Dutch through her big eyeglasses.

"Dutch, honey, is this the right church?"

"No, Mom, it's not the right church. This is Montana. Didn't anyone tell you?"

"I told her," Sis insists. She taps her temple with her finger and mouths, "Not doing well."

"Why didn't we just have it at our church?" says Mom.

Dutch looks at me with a scowl and says, "I don't know, Mom."

The funeral director's introduces himself. His name is Pete Weiss. Skinny guy, no hair. He wants us all in the chapel, but wives and kids swarm past him and down the hallways, checking out the kitchen, lining up outside the bathrooms.

Within fifteen minutes, Val's grandkids find some nursery toys and start up a game of dodgeball in a side room. Pete Weiss tries to break it up, but he takes a direct hit to the lips instead. The kids tell him he's out. He checks his mouth for blood and comes to Dutch.

"We can't have these kids playing with a ball in here," he says.

Dutch storms in and says, "You kids simmer down, give me that ball, and clear the hell out of here."

They follow his instructions—quickly, and in the order they were issued.

He turns to Pete Weiss and says, "Pardon my language, pastor."

"I'm not the pastor," he says. "I'm the funeral director."

"Oh," says Dutch, eyeing the guy like he might be a pretender to that title, too. "Then, never mind."

We filter into the chapel and talk about our flights and drive time. Mom's irritated. Word is she may have forgotten that Dad is dead. Pete Weiss says he'll be in soon to walk us through the schedule, but he can't seem to get off the phone.

It's a small church house with only one set of lavatories. After one hour, the ladies' room is clean out of toilet paper. Everyone knows it was Larry and his family. They all have toilet problems—Larry's got a bashful bladder and Arlene can't sneeze without peeing her pants. Their kids all inherited the same disorders. Everywhere they go they spend half their time in the toilet.

Dutch summons Pete Weiss with a little horse whistle.

"A gaggle of our ladyfolk came in from Rexburg today," says Dutch. "Been driving since three this morning. They decimated the ladies' room TP. Where can we get our hands on a couple more rolls?"

"I don't know," he says, putting a hand over his phone. "I'm here from Billings."

Dutch sighs powerfully, points at his sons and me and a few others, and leads us into the foyer, where he arranges us into search parties.

"We're looking for a supply closet and-or a janitor's room. Move out."

I stay behind. Larry gets the idea to roll some toilet paper from the men's room onto the empty tube from the ladies'. Guilt will do that—make you think something like that is a good idea. Or maybe he's done this before. He sets up a two-man system with his half-asleep teenage son, Taylor.

"Keep it straight," he scolds. "This will only work if it's straight." Taylor yawns.

Larry turns to me and says, "So, James, word is you know why the big change in plans."

I shrug. He doesn't push it. Dutch shows up with his searchers.

"Oh, Larry, you're kidding me," says Dutch. He rubs his face, adjusts his tie.

"Leave us be," says Larry.

"We found the closet, knucklehead, but it's locked." He goes into the chapel and says, "Listen up, folks. Who here can pick a lock?"

Val comes over. He looks down at me like an owl on a phone pole.

"How you doing, kid?" he says. He's bent over in his trademark slouch.

"I'm okay. You?"

"Everyone's saying Dad told you why he wanted to be buried way out here. What's the old man up to, Jimmy?"

"He gave me a letter just before he went into the hospital. Told me to read it at the cemetery."

"He's messing with us, isn't he? Did he sell the Place? Just tell me. I won't say anything."

"At the cemetery. Dad's wishes, not mine."

Val grins like he already knows what's going on, but he's not slouching anymore. It's his way of backing down. He's twenty years older than me and a foot taller, but he's backing down. I can't believe it. It's like Dad's standing behind me in his overalls and work boots.

When I was three years old, Val went into the Air Force. Then Bill went to college back east, and Dutch went into the Army. Dad cursed them—in their bedrooms while they packed, in the driveway as they loaded their trucks.

"I need you on the Place," he said. "What am I supposed to do out here with no help?"

They didn't listen. When Dad broke down and got a hired hand, Larry and Stu quit showing up for chores. Dad kicked them, threw feed buckets at them, but after awhile they left, too. That's when Dad started threatening to sell the Place out from under us.

"You don't know what you got here," he'd yelled at them on the phone. "This is land, the only real thing there is. I'll sell it all before I give it to you deadbeats. Sell it and buy two hundred acres of bare ground somewhere. Make you start over."

They didn't believe him back then, or they didn't care. Now, as we sit there in the chapel, I catch them looking at me.

Pete Weiss finally hangs up his phone and comes in. He can't work the microphone, so he tries talking over everyone. I hear about every other word. What time things start, who's supposed to be where. I think about Dad's letter. How I'll read it. I don't want to rush it.

Pete Weiss tells the pallbearers to stand up, so we do.

Before Dad died, it never occurred to me that he had exactly the right number of sons to bear him to the grave. Six sons to carry his casket, one daughter to stay with his widow. Like he'd planned it that way, like maybe that would keep us around.

Pete Weiss takes the six of us into the viewing room for a dry run. The casket sits on a gurney that we can roll into the chapel, but from there to the hearse we've got to horse it up some stairs and across a lawn.

Dutch says, "That figures."

Dad always joked about being buried in a pine box, so Val built him an old-timey coffin. It's pine, but dark-stained and lacquered. The hinges and braces are from old barns and buckboards. The handles are made of bent horseshoes. Val's been in cabinetmaking since he got out of the military, and this is easily his finest work. He runs his hand along the coping. His eyes turn wet, though whether it's because we're burying Dad or the casket, I can't say.

Pete Weiss positions us around the casket according to height and estimated lifting ability. Val and Bill are tallest, at the front. I'm across from Dutch, on the middle handles. Larry and Stu are behind us.

"The key is to breathe," says Pete Weiss. "Breathe deeply and steadily. Don't hurry. Guys in the front set the pace. So. Let's lift him up so we can get an idea of the weight. Any questions?"

"Yeah," grumbles Dutch out of the side of his mouth, "what's this 'we' business?"

Dad weighed less than two hundred pounds when he died. The

casket's at least another hundred and fifty pounds. It should be about sixty pounds each, but it's more than that, a lot more, and we're lifting it with one hand. The worse thing is the horseshoe handles—they cut into our fingers and squish our hands until our knuckles overlap. Everyone winces.

"These handles worked great while it was empty," grunts Val.

We tell him not to worry about it, but we set the casket down right away.

After lunch, we take our places around the church for the viewing. Val stands by Dad. Pete Weiss posts a couple grandkids outside the doors as ushers. He puts Dutch in the foyer to direct traffic, as if Dutch wouldn't go out there anyway.

Then we wait, but no one comes. An hour goes by. Nobody. The grandkid-ushers abandon their stations. The other kids slip outside and play tag in the howling wind.

Val moved away to Maryland while he was in the Air Force. Bill's been in Texas so long he sounds like he's from there. Dutch moved all around in the army, but never back to Idaho. Larry and Stu stayed around but never worked the Place. Dad kept on threatening until it became obvious no one was going to come back to work. After that it turned into a family joke.

One year at Thanksgiving, Val and Dutch were really riding him about it.

"Two hunnerd acres a' bare ground!" said Val, doing his best impression of Dad.

We all laughed.

"Where was it gonna be?" chuckled Dutch. "South Dakota?"

"Siberia," said Stu.

"Montana," said Dad, slamming down a big bowl of yams. He wasn't laughing. "I know just where, too. You laugh, but I wasn't joking then and I'm not now. I could still do it. Leave you with nothing but bare earth, like when great granddad started out."

"Doesn't make any sense, Dad," said Val, still half-kidding. "If you think we'll sell this place, why wouldn't we sell two hundred acres someplace else?"

"Oh Val, you're so damn smart," Dad snapped back, and the kidding was over. "You ever own any real property? Ever try to buying or selling it? No. It takes a toll on you. Makes you so you can't trust anybody. It eats up your time—thinking about it, working on it. No matter how much you get for it, you feel like you settled for less. This is real. This is important."

Val and Dutch were quiet.

"If you ever sell the Place," said Dad, "there'll be a house on every single acre within ten years. You won't be laughing then."

We wheel Dad into the chapel for the funeral. No one else comes. It's just us, but that's nearly a hundred people, and it's everyone— every one of Mom and Dad's kids, grandkids, and great-grands. It's like a miracle. People are crying, laughing, hugging.

We settle into the pews and Dutch runs the show. He talks, Sis talks, Larry's girls sing a song. Considering it's a funeral everyone's pretty happy, but word has gotten around about the letter.

Dutch looks at me from the pulpit. Looks at me for a few seconds, then says, "Anybody got anything to say before we head out? It's a good forty-five minutes to the cemetery."

Everyone cranes around to look at me. Val jerks his head at the pulpit. I don't answer.

"Fine," says Dutch. "Let's take the old man for a ride."

We line up around the casket and lift, grunting, trying to get in step. My whole arm is throbbing before we're even outside. Pete Weiss opens the side doors and wind whips into the chapel. If anything, it's blowing harder now. In the parking lot we catch grit in our eyes and teeth. We get Dad in the hearse and then stand in the wind, shaking out our clawed-up hands, and rubbing them.

Pete Weiss says he was worried about the handles on the casket all along but didn't want to say anything. Dutch looks like he's going to sock him in the mouth.

"But I called the caretaker," Pete Weiss assures us. "He's got a four-wheeler we can use to get the casket to the plot."

"My dad is not going to his grave on some old four-wheeler," says Dutch flexing his hand. "It's not that bad. We'll carry it."

"No," laughs Pete Weiss. "No, the plot is smack-dab in the middle of the section. It's a long way. Twice as far as this at least."

"We'll carry it," says Dutch.

It's more than twice as far.

We take Dad halfway, then set him down to rest our hands. Dutch's fat knuckles are bright red. The caretaker sits on his four-wheeler shaking his head. Wind rips around the cemetery, blowing hats and programs. The sun is coming low. Everyone's waiting at the plot, and the hot wind is blowing, so we swap sides and pick Dad up again.

"What's in the letter, James?" hisses Val as we pick our way between the gravestones.

"When we get there," I grunt.

"He sold it, didn't he?"

"When we get there."

When Dad is at the winch, our wives pat our backs and help us to our seats.

I pull the letter from my pocket. My hands are burning and cramped so bad I have trouble unfolding the paper. I've already read it two dozen times—I helped Dad write it. But it looks different now, like some ancient prophecy.

Dad's instructions have the chairs facing east. I'm standing up and facing west, with Dad's grave between me and everyone else. They all look at me. I look at the letter. I don't rush it.

"I never was going to sell the Place," I read.

Moans and gasps. Bill leans back in his chair, face to the sky. Val pinches the bridge of his nose. Dutch looks like he's going to sock me in the mouth.

Val was the first to say it out loud—that Dad went crazy after we all left. Dad leased out the land and went to auctions and estate sales to keep himself busy. He bought up saddles, tack, old farm equipment. He piled it up around the house. When there were no auctions he'd order things off TV—gadgets, dietary supplements, so-called collector's items. He bought big bronze statues of horses and eagles and Indians.

One year when we came home for Christmas the house was so crowded with bronze statuary and exercise equipment we had trouble finding places to sit down. Val told us we ought to do something about it.

"Go ahead and try," said Dutch.

So Val said, "Dad, about alla this stuff. You can't just—"

"Can't what?" said Dad. "Spend all my money? Why not? Still mine. Don't worry, I'll be out of your way faster than you think."

The letter rattles in my hand like a kite. I read the next line.

"But if I was to sell the Place and buy some bare ground to start over, this is where it would be."

I look up at them. Mom's eyes are clear.

"Now," I continue, "get on your feet and take a look around."

They trade glances.

I tell them, "He wants you to stand up and turn around."

They do it. One at a time, relieved. Val puts his hands in his pants pockets and eases into his slouch. We look out past the foot of the cemetery hill and the valley below. The sun touches the hills. The Mussleshell River shines like a ribbon of tinsel.

"That is it," reads the letter. "That is the two-hundred acres out there. It's federal land now. It wasn't back then. They graze cows on it and there's some oil wells. But I like to think this is what our Place looked like a couple hundred years ago, before the fields, before the roads. I'm sure you can see it. The way the hills kindly lean back on their haunches, the river coming down between."

Everyone is quiet. I'm not reading the letter anymore. Dad is.

"Nobody showed up, did they? Nobody drove six hours to see an old crank planted. If we were in Boise you'd have the usual suspects. Violet Nielson asking how you're doing every five minutes. She'd bring that rotten spaghetti casserole of hers. Not even the dog would eat it."

"He's right about that," says Mom with a shrug and nod.

"Olive Inverness would play 'Nearer My God To Thee' so slow you'd feel yourself getting older, getting closer to Him whether you wanted to or not. Then Vic Olsen would show up in that infernal track suit of his to gloat that he's five years older than me and still getting around. Tell you how many miles he can jog. But they didn't come. It's just us."

It seems hardly possible, but the wind picks up again. We all stand looking. Arms go to waists.

"I was wrong," says Dad. "There is only one thing that is real, but it's not land. I learned that much before I went. You all can go on home now. Watch over Mother for me. She becomes cranky some mornings."

"Right again," says Mom. We laugh.

"I'll hang back and watch over this valley. Me and James came here in April. While he was writing a check for the plot I came out and looked out over the valley and saw the ghosts of outlaws and Indians and bison passing by."

Mom leans into Sis with a mighty sob. Sis holds her up. Val and Dutch come to her side.

"I expect you'll sell the Place, and they'll cut up the land for backyards and parking lots. The money will go for college degrees and new cars. It's the way of things. I have made my peace by it. Then again, you may want to start again. You may want to work the Place. If this is so, I'll rest easier still. And if you want to start over, say you started here."

RESERVATION

Lorraine Jeffery

"Walk in beauty."
"I try old one (shi' cheii)"

Dusty roads to four
       sacred mountains.
Cans and paper caught
       in gray sagebrush
Gritty wind blasts
       rusty trucks,
       hot mummified seats,
       wheels gone.

Mesas, plateaus and red rock,
       belong to Washington.
       Black words in a book.

Navajo Nation,
Mother Earth, Father Sky and the Diné.
"The land belongs to no one," he sings.

"Your clan,"
       Calloused feet stomping,
       step, touch, step touch.
       Sandpaint the locust–first one on earth.
       Walmart blanket warms.
            Sell the woven one,
            kachina design.

Wail of the hatáál
     "A Blessingway?"

"No."
     Mesquite fences cannot hold
     a chant that turns to rap.
     "Shi' Cheii" (I try old one),
     but the car outruns the wind.